God with Us

Also by Daniel R. Hyde

How Can Justification Make Me Joyful?

Why Should I Fast?

Planting, Watering, Growing: Planting Confessionally Reformed Churches in the 21st Century, ed. with Shane Lems

In Defense of the Descent: A Response to Contemporary Critics

God with Us

KNOWING THE MYSTERY OF WHO JESUS IS

Second Edition

Daniel R. Hyde

Reformation Heritage Books
Grand Rapids, Michigan

God with Us
© 2007, 2021 by Daniel R. Hyde

All rights reserved. First edition 2007. Second edition 2021. No part of this book may be used or reproduced in any manner whatsoever without written permission except in the case of brief quotations embodied in critical articles and reviews. Direct your requests to the publisher at the following addresses:

Reformation Heritage Books
3070 29th St. SE
Grand Rapids, MI 49512
616-977-0889
orders@heritagebooks.org
www.heritagebooks.org

Unless otherwise indicated, Scripture taken from the New King James Version®. Copyright © 1982 by Thomas Nelson. Used by permission. All rights reserved.

Chapter 7 originally appeared as "Who Do Men Say That I Am? The Christ of the Qu'ran vs. the Christ of the Bible," *Christian Renewal* (April 12, 2004): 20–23, and is used by permission.

Unless otherwise indicated, emphases in quotations have been added by the author.

Printed in the United States of America
21 22 23 24 25 26/10 9 8 7 6 5 4 3 2 1

Library of Congress Cataloging-in-Publication Data

Names: Hyde, Daniel R., author.
Title: God with us : knowing the mystery of who Jesus is / Daniel R. Hyde.
Description: Second edition. | Grand Rapids, MI : Reformation Heritage Books,
 [2021] | Includes bibliographical references and index.
Identifiers: LCCN 2021011046 (print) | LCCN 2021011047 (ebook) |
 ISBN 9781601788658 (paperback) | ISBN 9781601788665 (epub)
Subjects: LCSH: Jesus Christ—History of doctrines.
Classification: LCC BT198 .H93 2021 (print) | LCC BT198 (ebook) | DDC
 232/.8—dc23
LC record available at https://lccn.loc.gov/2021011046
LC ebook record available at https://lccn.loc.gov/2021011047

For additional Reformed literature, request a free book list from Reformation Heritage Books at the above regular or email address.

Contents

Preface to the Second Edition vii

Introduction: Why You Need to Know Who Jesus Is...... 1
1. An Event like No Other 21
2. The God Who Is Also Man: Christ's Two Natures 39
3. The Son of God: Christ's Divine Nature............... 54
4. The Son of Man: Christ's Human Nature.............. 79
5. The God-Man: Christ's Single Person................. 104
6. The Importance of This Mysterious Doctrine 118
7. The Christ of the Qur'an versus the Christ of the Bible.. 135

Appendix 1: The Ecumenical Creeds 157
Appendix 2: The Seven Ecumenical Councils 167
Appendix 3: The Tome of Leo I 169
Scripture Index.. 179
Confessions Index 184

Preface to the Second Edition

Greatly satisfied that the first printing of this book was so well received and after several years of its being out of print, I have updated it for a second edition at the publisher's request. We are all products of a lifetime of experiences. This is no truer than when we read Scripture, meditate on it, and seek to write down some of its ideas on paper. Thankfully, the expertise and experiences of others teach us how to step outside our finite view of things in order to gather additional information from various points of view. Several readers and reviewers have given me invaluable feedback on how to make the book better in the years since its original publication. Of note were the reviews at *Reformation21* and in *Clarion*, the *Covenanter Review*, and the *Puritan Reformed Journal*. I thank those reviewers.

I desire to thank all those who have taken my membership classes at the Oceanside United Reformed Church over the past twenty years. These classes always include my feeble attempts to explain the profound mysteries of Jesus Christ contained in this book. Whether you are a dear old saint or a baby Christian, your insightful and timely questions have given me the building blocks of what I have written here. I especially wish to thank my long-time friend and theological sharpening stone, Dr. David VanDrunen, for originally encouraging me to seek a publisher for this material. As always, I am indebted to my wife, Karajean—my best friend, the mother of my children, my conversation partner, and my most honest (harshest!) critic. Apart from you, I could not make it through this earthly pilgrimage. Finally, my sons Cyprian James, Caiden Daniel, and Daxton Jeremiah and my daughter, Sadie Jean, teach me every day something of the wonder Mary must have experienced in raising her child—yet hers was also the Lord. I've prayed every day for you that you'd never know a day outside the love of Jesus!

Venite adoremus Dominum.

INTRODUCTION

Why You Need to Know Who Jesus Is

Imagine you're a sophomore at a Christian college. You came to the saving knowledge of Jesus Christ only three years earlier. You're in a chapel service. The guest speaker is explaining the marvelous event we Christians call the incarnation—the conception and birth of the eternal Son of God in human flesh. "It goes a little something like this," he says. "God came to earth and took on a human body." While speaking, he illustrates what that process of taking on a human body must have involved by picking up his coat, which lay over a choir pew behind him, and putting it on.

Shifting scenes: you're now in a Southern California beach city on a summer Saturday morning. Thousands of evangelical Christians have gathered for the "March for Jesus" celebration to walk through the city with praise music blaring from loudspeakers attached to the tops of vans and trucks. There are Christian T-shirts aplenty proudly worn; there's a sense of evangelistic purpose and zeal. In the midst of the crowd, you see a group of men holding up an enormous sign on poles: "Jesus: All God In A Bod."

These examples from my early Christian life illustrate that every one of us, from theologian to novice, have some way of explaining what the Bible says about Jesus being both God and man, about the Son of God becoming a man. The explanations above are imprecise, unhelpful, and even incorrect ways of expressing this biblical truth. The Son didn't wrap His eternal divinity in temporal humanity like a coat. He didn't park His divinity in a "bod" like a car in a garage.

Constrained by Culture

These examples are symbolic of a much larger problem within contemporary American Christianity. Just as a fish is constrained by water without knowing it, we've become constrained so much by our broader culture and Christian subculture that we don't even know it.[1] The problem is that the foundational doctrines of Scripture, as understood in the history of the Christian church, are rarely taught or preached in so much of American evangelicalism.[2] When they are, they're often presented without precision. This is the result of generations of preaching in many churches with the intent of simply making converts rather than disciples. Instead of emphasizing discipleship, pastors and their churches have been in a rush to convert as many people as possible before

---

1. For an entry into modern Western culture, see Charles Taylor, *Sources of the Self: The Making of the Modern Identity* (Cambridge, Mass.: Harvard University Press, 1989); and *A Secular Age* (Cambridge, Mass.: Harvard University Press, 2007).

2. On the somewhat amorphous term "evangelical/evangelicalism," see Mark Noll, "Defining Evangelicalism," in *Global Evangelicalism: Theology, History and Culture in Regional Perspective*, ed. Donald M. Lewis and Richard V. Pierard (Downers Grove, Ill.: InterVarsity Press, 2014), 17–37; Thomas S. Kidd, *Who Is an Evangelical? The History of a Movement in Crisis* (New Haven, Conn.: Yale University Press, 2019).

Introduction

Jesus returns. The gospel message has been turned into a watered-down, feel-good "Christianity." The method used by many pastors is evangelism by accommodation, giving converts "relevant," practical sermons about how to live day by day with purpose.

Jesus's command in the Great Commission is to "make disciples"—followers and students of Christ. Jesus then explains what He means by using the words "go," "baptizing," and "teaching" (Matt. 28:19–20). "After all," the reasoning goes, "it's not important to understand *how* Jesus Christ is both God and man; it's vital only that we live our lives for Him. It's not important to know things about Him—just to know Him." But who is He? Many Christians have been deceived into thinking that what they and the world need is a "practical" Christianity, not a "doctrinal" faith. Sadly, this attitude among self-professed, Bible-believing, evangelical Christians shows how far adrift Protestant evangelicalism has gone.

Delighting in Doctrine

What do I mean by this critique of Protestant evangelicals? The attitudes of "conservative" evangelicals today were precisely the ideas that Protestant *liberals* had in the early 1920s, which the Presbyterian minister and professor J. Gresham Machen (1881–1937) wrote so vigorously against.[3] Those who promote the strange union of liberalism and evangelicalism believe that doctrine is for only the academic community to

---

3. For an explanation and refutation of this type of thinking in the early 1920s, see J. Gresham Machen, *Christianity and Liberalism* (1923; repr., Grand Rapids: Eerdmans, 1994), 17–53.

debate and has no relevance for the daily life of the ordinary believer. "Doctrine divides," we're told, "but love for the Lord unites." As church-growth guru Rick Warren said in response to the question, "What is your dream?": "I'm looking for a second reformation. The first reformation of the church 500 years ago was about beliefs. This one is going to be about behavior. The first one was about creeds. This one is going to be about deeds. It is not going to be about what does the church believe, but about what is the church doing."[4] It's not surprising, then, that the best evangelicalism can do is produce a "Christian" culture of bumper stickers, sound-bite theology, and "witness wear" T-shirts and wristbands. Is it any wonder, then, that the esteemed J. I. Packer (1926–2020) once wrote that American evangelical Christianity is "3,000 miles wide and half an inch deep"?[5]

Truth be told, understanding doctrine isn't a man-made exercise for the elite but results from obeying God's commands to study and meditate on what He's revealed of Himself in His Word. For example, in the Pastoral Epistles, the apostle Paul wrote to two young pastors, Timothy and Titus, exhorting them that to teach and defend creeds was to promote deeds. He emphasized the importance of doctrine, calling it:

Good doctrine (1 Tim. 4:6)
Sound doctrine (1 Tim. 1:10; 2 Tim. 4:3; Titus 2:1)

---

4. David Kuo, "Rick Warren's Second Reformation," Beliefnet, accessed January 8, 2021, http://www.beliefnet.com/faiths/Christianity/2005/10/Rick-Warrens-Second-Reformation.aspx?p=1.

5. J. I. Packer, *A Quest for Godliness: The Puritan Vision of the Christian Life* (Wheaton, Ill.: Crossway, 1990), 22.

> That good thing which was committed to you (2 Tim. 1:14)
> The doctrine which accords with godliness (1 Tim. 6:3)
> The truth which accords with godliness (Titus 1:1)
> The faithful word (Titus 1:9)
> The pattern of sound words (2 Tim. 1:13)
> The mystery of the faith (1 Tim. 3:9)
> The words of faith (1 Tim. 4:6)
> Wholesome words (1 Tim. 6:3)

Doctrine, then, is simply biblical teaching that's food for the soul like good food for the body. Because of the New Testament's insistence on doctrine as set forth in the Pastoral Epistles, Machen said, "The Christian movement at its inception was not just a way of life in the modern sense, but a way of life founded upon a message."[6] The earliest Christian church's life of love and fellowship—in which believers had "all things in common," "sold their possessions and goods," and shared "among all, as anyone had need" (Acts 2:44–45)—was founded on their dedication to "the apostles' *doctrine*" (v. 42). John warned his audience not to welcome certain people into their homes based on their doctrine: "Whosoever transgresses and does not abide in the *doctrine of Christ* does not have God. He who abides in the *doctrine of Christ* has both the Father and the Son. If anyone comes to you and does not bring *this doctrine*, do not receive him into your house nor greet him" (2 John 9–10).

What we call doctrine, or theology, offers the only solid foundation on which a believer in Jesus Christ can reliably

---

6. Machen, *Christianity and Liberalism*, 21.

live the Christian life and face temptations and trials in their lives. The pattern of the New Testament Epistles evidences that Christian doctrine was first proclaimed and then applied to Christian living. This is clearly the structure of the book of Romans. Paul proclaims both the doctrine of people's sin and the doctrine of God's salvation in chapters 1:18–11:33, and then he applies those doctrines to life in the church and in the world in chapters 12:1–15:33. Doctrine and life are inseparably united. B. B. Warfield (1851–1921), the great Princeton theologian, lamented that in his day, not unlike our own, many so-called Christian theologians were rejecting the historic Christian doctrine of the two natures of Christ. This is a doctrine that I'll explain in this book which teaches that our Lord Jesus Christ is both God and man. Instead of this teaching, liberal Christian churches in Warfield's day were calling for a more "relevant" Christianity. To this Warfield said, "The doctrine of the Two Natures is only another way of stating the doctrine of the Incarnation; and the doctrine of the Incarnation is the hinge on which the Christian system turns. No Two Natures, no Incarnation; no Incarnation, no Christianity in any distinctive sense."[7]

Renewing Your Mind

The spirit of this age is to feel rather than to think.[8] As Christians, we're called by God to be "transformed by the renewing

---

7. B. B. Warfield, "The 'Two Natures' and Recent Christological Speculation," in *Christology and Criticism, The Works of Benjamin B. Warfield* (1932; repr., Grand Rapids: Baker Book House, 2000), 3:259.

8. See, for example, William Davies, *Nervous States: Democracy and the Decline of Reason* (2018; repr., New York: W. W. Norton, 2020).

of your mind" instead of being "conformed to this world"—that is, the spirit of the age in which we live (Rom. 12:2). In the words of the African American pastor Charles Octavius Boothe (1845–1924), "Before the charge 'know thyself' [exemplified in this spirit of our age] ought to come the far greater charge, 'know thy God.'"[9] One of the ways in which the church has been conformed to this age is adopting pragmatism in the form of a relevant, user-friendly religion. The apostle Paul characterized us before our life in Christ as having a futile mind; a darkened understanding; an ignorant, blind, unfeeling (callous; ESV) heart; and an impure life (Eph. 4:17–19). Now, however, our behavior is transformed, and we're "light in the Lord" (5:8). Enlightened by the gospel and the work of the Holy Spirit, we undergo a metamorphosis, as Paul described in Romans 12:2. Jesus commands us to love God not just with our hearts but also with our minds (Matt. 22:37). This is a part of the lifetime work of putting off the old self of sin while putting on the new self, "renewed in knowledge according to the image of Him who created him" (Col. 3:10).

Knowing to Know

What does this mean for the topic of this book? It means we must come to realize that without understanding who Jesus Christ is as God and man (what we call His *person*), we'll be left puzzled about what He has done for us (what we call His *work*).[10] Simply put, how can we know Jesus as Savior and

---

9. Charles Octavius Boothe, *Plain Theology for Plain People* (1890; repr., Bellingham, Wash.: Lexham, 2017), 4.

10. G. C. Berkouwer, *The Person of Christ*, Studies in Dogmatics, trans. John Vriend (Grand Rapids: Eerdmans, 1954), 105.

Lord unless we know something about Him? In our Western culture, people do not select spouses before they know the personality, strengths, and weaknesses of the other person. In a similar manner, we must know God. The first question of the Westminster Shorter Catechism (1647) states that our chief end and purpose in life is to "enjoy [God] forever."[11] The first question of the Heidelberg Catechism (1563) states that our only comfort is the assurance that we belong to Jesus Christ, "body and soul, both in life and in death."[12] Most assuredly, our only way to recognize what God has done for us is to come to a firm understanding of who He is.

When we understand who Jesus is, we conclude that He's absolutely essential. Knowledge of who Jesus is leads those who already have a relationship with Him to know Him more deeply. If you've not placed your trust, hope, and love in the Lord, it's necessary to come to know Him this way in the first place before your relationship with Him can grow. The big point of this book is that we must clearly understand that Jesus Christ is fully God and fully man. If Jesus Christ is not God, then He can't be the Savior, for only God saves. Furthermore, if He's not God, then He can't hear our prayers. On the other hand, if Jesus isn't human, then He can't be our Savior because only a human can pay for the sins that humans committed before God in Paradise (Genesis 3). In addition, if He's not human, then He can't sympathize with us in our weaknesses. Finally, if the divine and human natures in Jesus Christ aren't united in one person, He can't be our

---

11. Philip Schaff, ed., *The Creeds of Christendom*, rev. David S. Schaff (1931; repr., Grand Rapids: Baker Books, 1996), 3:676.

12. Schaff, *Creeds*, 3:307.

Savior because He's neither God nor man, but a third entity. He wouldn't be completely God or completely man.

The relation of factual knowledge to relational knowledge is also essential for expressing our faith. If we profess to believe in Jesus Christ, then we must express this belief. As the great Dutch theologian Herman Bavinck (1854–1921) said, "If we believe that we have the Christ, that we have communion with Him, that we are His own, then such belief must be confessed with the mouth and be spoken in words, terms, expressions, and descriptions of some kind or other."[13]

Our faith must have expression in words, yet we can only express this faith if we have certain knowledge about who our Lord is. In order to pray, to bless the Lord with all our hearts, and to tell the world about Him, we must have a foundational knowledge of who He is and what He has done for us.[14] This knowledge, then, is of a great mystery, a knowledge that pilgrims have in this life, and a knowledge that the catholic (universal) church in all times and in all places has expressed for millennia.

Holy Mystery

Our knowledge of Jesus Christ is not merely an intellectual or theoretical exercise, though. The biblical words for "know" in both Hebrew (*yada*) and Greek (*ginosko*) denote also an

---

13. Herman Bavinck, *Our Reasonable Faith*, trans. Henry Zylstra (Grand Rapids: Eerdmans, 1956), 322.

14. On the necessity of confessing our faith as members of the body of Christ in terms of the church's historic creeds and confessions, see Daniel R. Hyde, *The Good Confession: An Exploration of the Christian Faith* (Eugene, Ore.: Wipf & Stock, 2006), 7–28.

intimate relationship—hence the traditional language of a man "knowing" his wife. Jesus spoke this way: "And this is eternal life, that they may *know* You, the only true God, and Jesus Christ whom You have sent" (John 17:3). While a husband's knowledge of his wife or a friend's knowledge of a friend is comprehensible because it's creature to creature, knowing God, by definition, is mysterious. So unlike a husband knowing his wife, the knowledge of God is just that—knowing *God*, the Creator of the universe. Such knowledge brings us to an experience of holy mystery. He's God, we're not; He's Creator, we're mere creatures. For example, when the apostle John entered into the presence of the ascended Christ, as recorded in the Revelation of Himself, John was humbled and awed in silence: "And when I saw Him, I fell at His feet as dead" (Rev. 1:17). Throughout the Scriptures, we see this same effect on those who enter into the holy, mysterious presence of our mighty Savior, whether on Moses, who hid his face and was afraid to look up before the burning bush (Ex. 3:1–6); or on Isaiah, who cried out that he was unclean in the midst of the Lord in His heavenly temple (Isa. 6:1–7).

Amazingly, connecting with God is no different for us now than it was for Moses, Isaiah, and John when we open the Bible and seek to learn about the Lord Jesus through reading its pages. Through the medium of the Holy Scriptures, the Holy Spirit powerfully brings us into the very holy and mysterious presence of Jesus Christ Himself. The Scriptures speak of Christ (John 5:39; 1 Peter 1:10–12) and are used like a sword to pierce our inmost being (Heb. 4:12). When we study the sublime mysteries of the faith, such as the incarnation and two natures of Christ as revealed in the Scriptures, we approach

Christ Himself. When we do this, we subject ourselves to His living and active word, just like Moses, Isaiah, and John before the Lord in glory.

Because of this, it's of the utmost importance to study the subject of this book, Jesus Christ, and the mysteries of who He is with reverence and humility. One of the great leaders of the Protestant Reformation, John Calvin (1509–1564), advised his readers to have this attitude toward this subject: "It is very easy to see how beautifully they [Christ's two natures—divine and human] accord with each other, provided they have a sober interpreter, one who examines these great mysteries with the reverence which is meet."[15] Let's turn to the Bible with reverence and with awe. Let's turn to it with heartfelt prayer: "Blessed Lord, who hast caused all holy Scriptures to be written for our learning: Grant that we may in such wise hear them, read, mark, learn, and inwardly digest them, that by patience and comfort of thy holy Word, we may embrace, and ever hold fast, the blessed hope of everlasting life, which thou hast given us in our Saviour Jesus Christ. Amen."[16]

Pilgrim Theology

Like Calvin, we must be sober and reverent when considering both the great, holy mystery of the incarnation and how the divine and human relate to each other in our Lord. As we study the Bible and seek to understand it, one of the ways

---

15. John Calvin, *Institutes of the Christian Religion*, ed. John T. McNeill, trans. Ford Lewis Battles (Philadelphia: Westminster Press, 1960), 2.14.4.

16. "The Collect for the Second Sunday in Advent," *The Book of Common Prayer* (2004; repr., Cambridge: Cambridge University Press, 2012), 49. This is the standard edition of 1662.

we can be sober and reverent is by realizing that we have a pilgrim theology. In classic Reformed theological categories, we speak of two kinds of theology: original (also called *archetypal*) and derived (also called *ectypal*). Original theology is theology as the Creator knows it, while derived theology is theology as creatures know it—whether the angels, the people of God in heaven who see our Lord face-to-face (1 Cor. 13:12; 1 John 3:2; Rev. 22:4), or the people of God here on earth who are pilgrims.[17]

Scripture speaks of this basic distinction between God's knowledge and our knowledge. When Moses preached to the Israelites, he said, "The secret things belong to the LORD our God, but those things which are revealed belong to us and to our children forever, that we may do all the words of this law" (Deut. 29:29). God knows the secret things; we know only what He reveals. Later in the history of God's dealings with Israel, the LORD spoke through the prophet Isaiah in a similar way:

---

17. This classic distinction can be found in older writers, especially Franciscus Junius, *A Treatise on True Theology: With the Life of Franciscus Junius*, trans. David C. Noe (Grand Rapids: Reformation Heritage Books, 2014); as well as in more modern writers such as Louis Berkhof, *Systematic Theology* (1939; repr., Grand Rapids: Eerdmans, 1994), 34–35. For more on this distinction, see Richard A. Muller, *Post-Reformation Reformed Dogmatics: The Rise and Development of Reformed Orthodoxy, ca. 1520 to ca. 1725*, 2nd ed. (Grand Rapids: Baker Academic, 2003), 1:225–38; Willem van Asselt, "The Fundamental Meaning of Theology: Archetypal and Ectypal Theology in Seventeenth-Century Thought," *Westminster Theological Journal* 64 (2002): 319–35; R. Scott Clark, "Janus, the Well-Meant Offer of the Gospel and Westminster Theology," in *The Pattern of Sound Words: A Festschrift for Robert B. Strimple*, ed. David VanDrunen (Phillipsburg, N.J.: P&R, 2004), 149–80; R. Scott Clark, *Recovering the Reformed Confession: Our Theology, Piety, and Practice* (Phillipsburg, N.J.: P&R, 2008), 142–50.

> My thoughts are not your thoughts,
> Nor are your ways My ways....
> For as the heavens are higher than the earth,
> So are My ways higher than your ways,
> And My thoughts than your thoughts. (Isa. 55:8–9)

This distinction is also evident in Paul's words to the Corinthians: "For what man knows the things of a man except the spirit of the man which is in him? Even so no one knows the things of God except the Spirit of God" (1 Cor. 2:11).

This means we must confess that we don't know everything there is to know about God or our Lord Jesus Christ. Although the Holy Spirit has revealed much to us, "that we might know the things that have been freely given to us by God" (1 Cor. 2:12)—things that "belong to us…forever" (Deut. 29:29)—He's still enshrouded in much mystery.

Therefore, we must confess that our study of the Bible and deriving theology from it is our attempt to come as close as possible to God's "thoughts," or His theology. Our language, vocabulary, and descriptions of how God works will stretch our imaginations and souls as far as humanly possible. Bavinck described this feature of theological language: "The Christian church from the very beginning…confessed the most intimate, the profoundest, and therefore the altogether unique, communion of God and man. Its representatives in the earliest period sometimes expressed themselves in an awkward way. They had to struggle, first to form a somewhat clear notion of the reality, and then to give expression to this idea in clear language."[18]

---

18. Bavinck, *Our Reasonable Faith*, 319–20.

The American Dutch Reformed theologian Louis Berkhof (1873–1957) described this mystery of the incarnation and Christ's two natures in the dialogue of the early church: "The early Church did not claim to be able to penetrate to the depths of this great doctrine, and did not pretend to give a solution of the problem of the incarnation in the formula of Chalcedon. It merely sought to guard the truth against the errors of theorizers, and to give a formulation of it which would ward off various, palpably unscriptural, constructions of the truth."[19]

The point of saying all this is that we remember we are merely pilgrims, living "east of Eden" (Gen. 4:16; see also 3:24) in the wilderness. By faith, we're making our way toward the heavenly city, but we've not yet arrived. We must humbly confess that as pilgrims we rely on the Lord. As needy pilgrims, let us desire the heavenly manna of the Word, one crumb at a time, since "man shall not live by bread alone; but man lives by every word that proceeds from the mouth of the LORD" (Deut. 8:3). After Jesus's disciples abandoned Him and Jesus asked if His hand-chosen disciples would leave too, this is what Peter confessed: "Lord, to whom shall we go? You have the words of eternal life" (John 6:68). As Boothe said, "Let us not be unmindful of the fact that we vile, short-sighted worms should approach the solemn task of studying God with feelings of humility and awe. God is found of the lowly, but hides himself from the proud and self-sufficient man. When Daniel

---

19. Louis Berkhof, *The History of Christian Doctrines* (Grand Rapids: Baker Book House, 1937), 101–2.

fasted and prayed and made confession of sin, the secrets of the Lord were unfolded to his view."[20]

The Word of God is the source of our derived theology. When we read that "the secret things belong to the LORD our God" (Deut. 29:29) and "My thoughts are not your thoughts" (Isa. 55:8), we might easily be led to question whether we can really know anything about God at all. This is true. We can't know anything about God unless He reveals Himself to us. We find these revealed truths in "two books," to use a concept from the Belgic Confession of Faith (1561).

The first book of the knowledge of God is "the creation, preservation, and government of the universe" (art. 2). Paul says that because of our sinfulness (Rom. 1:18–32), this book is limited in its power. It can't lead a person to a saving knowledge of God, only to a sufficient knowledge that God exists: "All which things are sufficient to convince men and leave them without excuse" (art. 2).[21] The Westminster Confession of Faith (1647) speaks of the limits of this general revelation of God in creation as well: "Although the light of nature, and the works of creation and providence do so far manifest the goodness, wisdom, and power of God, as to leave men inexcusable; yet are they not sufficient to give that knowledge of God, and of his will, which is necessary unto salvation" (chap. 1.1).[22]

The second book is Scripture: "He makes Himself more clearly and fully known to us by His holy and divine Word, that is to say, as far as is necessary for us to know in this life,

---

20. Boothe, *Plain Theology for Plain People*, 4.
21. Schaff, *Creeds*, 3:384.
22. Schaff, *Creeds*, 3:600.

to His glory and our salvation" (art. 2).[23] About this book the Belgic Confession further explains:

> We confess that this Word of God was not sent nor delivered by the will of man, but that men spake from God, being moved by the Holy Spirit, as the apostle Peter says; and that afterwards God, from a special care which He has for us and our salvation, commanded His servants, the prophets and apostles, to commit His revealed word to writing; and He Himself wrote with His own finger the two tables of the law. Therefore we call such writings holy and divine Scriptures. (art. 3)[24]

Because of His "special care…for us," the Lord revealed His saving will and work through servants such as Moses in spoken and written forms. What the Belgic Confession calls God's "special care," the Westminster Confession elaborates further, saying, "Therefore it pleased the Lord, at sundry times, and in divers manners, to reveal himself, and to declare that his will unto his church; and afterwards, for the better preserving and propagating of the truth, and for the more sure establishment and comfort of the church against the corruption of the flesh, and the malice of Satan and of the world, to commit the same wholly unto writing" (ch. 1.1).[25]

Moses thus spoke of this written word as "those things which are revealed," those things that "belong to us and to

---

23. Schaff, *Creeds*, 3:384. On Belgic Confession, art. 2, see Daniel R. Hyde, *With Heart and Mouth: An Exposition of the Belgic Confession* (Grandville, Mich.: Reformed Fellowship, 2008), 53–62.

24. Schaff, *Creeds*, 3:384–85. On Belgic Confession, art. 3, see Hyde, *With Heart and Mouth*, 63–71.

25. Schaff, *Creeds*, 3:600–601.

our children forever." This truth brings us to a knowledge of salvation as God enters into a covenant relationship with us, but this truth also enables us to glorify the God who made and saved us, "that we may do all the words of this law" (Deut. 29:29).

Historic Catholicity

As pilgrims seeking to know the mysteries about the Lord Jesus Christ as best we can this side of glory, we join that great congregation in the wilderness throughout the ages, the people of God. The mystery of the incarnation was the hope preached by the old covenant prophets when they proclaimed the coming of Immanuel, God with us (Isa. 7:14). They looked for the Lord Himself, the One who saved their fathers from Egypt, to come to earth to aid His suffering people—again. How this occurred in all its detail was manifest in the new covenant as the Holy One Himself was born and named Jesus, meaning "the LORD saves" (see Matt. 1:21).

As the early church spread out in the wilderness of this world, they confessed that *the* Son of God became a man, all the while existing as coequal with the Father. While the Scriptures use the language "son of God" for those who aren't divine, such as Adam (Luke 3:38), Israel (Ex. 4:22; Jer. 31:9), and David (Ps. 89:20, 27), it reserves the language of *the* Son of God for God's eternal Son to demonstrate His divinity.

As Protestants, whether Reformed or Lutheran, we join the historic church in speaking of the Son as God. We stand shoulder to shoulder with the church catholic, east and west, confessing the wonderful doctrine of the incarnation. The Son of God became man. By doing so He effected a hypostatic union of His two natures: perfect God and perfect man. As Protestants, we're confessional Christians. We confess wholeheartedly the truths about the triune nature of God and the two natures of Jesus Christ as summarized in the great creeds of the ancient church—the Apostles' Creed, Nicene Creed (325/381), Athanasian Creed, and Definition of Chalcedon (451).[26] These truths were reaffirmed in the confessions of the Protestant Reformation, whether in the Reformed confessions, such as the Heidelberg Catechism, Belgic Confession, Thirty-Nine Articles (1571), Westminster Confession of Faith and Larger and Shorter Catechisms; or Lutheran confessions, such as the Augsburg Confession (1530) and Luther's Small and Large Catechisms (1529). As churches, we need to continue being historic, mindful of true catholicity in order to keep us in line with the truth but also to satisfy the longing in all our hearts for transcendence.

In this book we'll delight in doctrine. We'll renew our minds. We'll stand in awe of holy mystery. We'll walk on the path of pilgrim theology. We'll confess historic catholicity. Doing this will give us knowledge of the deep mystery of who Jesus is. As we come to a better understanding of this mystery, we'll come to know Him better. Knowing Him is salvation. We'll also apply this mystery to our comfort and confidence in our sufferings as pilgrims in this life, to our witness to the world, and to our worship before the throne of God's heavenly grace. If you don't believe in Jesus Christ (yet!), but are simply seeking to learn about Him, I pray this book causes you to consider His amazing claims and the mysteries about

---

26. See Appendix 1: The Ecumenical Creeds.

Him. In all this, our goal is to stand with that catholic cloud of witnesses (Heb. 12:1), the company which no man can number (Rev. 7:9) who have gone before us suffering even death for these doctrines, and confess "God with us."

ONE

An Event like No Other

> And suddenly there was with the angel a multitude of
> the heavenly host praising God and saying,
> > "Glory to God in the highest,
> > And on earth peace, goodwill toward men!"
> > —LUKE 2:13–14

Humanity lay in a coffin of its own making, being "dead in trespasses and sins" (Eph. 2:1). Men, women, and, sadly, children wallowed in the miry pit of their own sinful hearts and actions (Pss. 40:2; 51:1–12; Jer. 17:9). Their world was enshrouded in the darkness of unbelief and unrighteous living (Isa. 9:2; John 1:5). Their minds were blinded in futility (Eph. 4:17–18). Sin and its great consequence, death, were the spiritual conditions under which all humanity existed, under the bondage of him "who had the power of death, that is, the devil" (Heb. 2:14). No one was exempt.

The sin of the first man, Adam, and humanity's subsequent sins set the stage for the primary actor of the biblical narrative, God, "who is and who was and who is to come" (Rev. 1:8). The self-sufficient One who needs nothing beyond

Himself,[1] the Creator and Sustainer of all, the God who was sinned against was about to enter the drama of human history suddenly in a way He had never done before. God was pleased to pursue the pinnacle of His creation by becoming just like sinful humanity, except without sin. He entered this sinful world in order to bring the slaves of hell into heaven. To this, heaven's choirs could only sing, "Glory to God in the highest!" This is the gospel of the incarnation.

The Goal of History

The pitiful condition of humanity began sometime after "the beginning" (Gen. 1:1). The God who had said "and it was so" had been rejected. His most intimate creation, formed with His own hands "of the dust of the ground" and filled with His life-giving breath (Gen. 2:7; cf. Ps. 104:30) rebelled against Him. Made in His own image and likeness (Gen. 1:26–27), just "a little lower than the angels" and "crowned…with glory and honor" (Ps. 8:5), man and woman chose not to reflect that image but to undergo a makeover. They effaced God's image "by willful disobedience" (Heidelberg Catechism 9).[2] Sadly, humanity did not gratefully obey its Creator. It was in this condition "that our most gracious God, in his admirable wisdom and goodness, seeing that man had thus thrown himself into temporal and spiritual death, and made himself wholly

---

1. This is the attribute of God called *aseity*. See "aseitas" in Richard A. Muller, *Dictionary of Latin and Greek Theological Terms: Drawn Principally from Protestant Scholastic Theology*, 2nd ed. (Grand Rapids: Baker Academic, 2017), 41–42.

2. Schaff, *Creeds*, 3:310.

miserable, was pleased to seek and comfort him" (Belgic Confession, art. 17).[3]

The Goal in the Garden

Before sin entered the world, the Creator spoke the law: "Of the tree of the knowledge of good and evil you shall not eat, for in the day that you eat of it you shall surely die" (Gen. 2:17). After sin entered the world, the Creator spoke the "first gospel" (*protoeuangelion*; Gen. 3:15).[4] This gospel, or good news, was "first revealed in Paradise, afterwards proclaimed by the holy Patriarchs and Prophets, and foreshadowed by the sacrifices and other ceremonies of the law, and finally fulfilled by his well-beloved Son" (Heidelberg Catechism 19).[5] It promised a seed from Eve who would bruise the head of the seed of the serpent, who is "the great dragon…that serpent of old, called the Devil and Satan, who deceives the whole world" (Rev. 12:9). This promise, then, became the *telos*, the goal, of human history. Already in the garden there was an eschatology—a goal to which everything is moving. That goal was "the revelation of Jesus Christ" (Rev. 1:1 ESV). History rushed toward its purpose to bring forth the Redeemer for sinful man.

---

3. Schaff, *Creeds*, 3:402. On Belgic Confession, art. 17, see Hyde, *With Heart and Mouth*, 221–30.

4. Also called the "mother promise" (*moederbelofte*) by Dutch theologians. For example, see Herman Bavinck, *Magnalia Dei: Onderwijzing in de Christelijke Religie naar Gereformeerde Belijdenis* (Kampen: J. H. Kok, 1909), 15, 301, 305, 320, 598.

5. Schaff, *Creeds*, 3:313.

The Goal in the Narratives

If it's the case that the true "purpose driven life" was that of Eve's seed, Jesus Christ, and that history was awaiting the fulfillment of this promise, we need to recognize the profound effect this has for how we read the story of the Old Testament. Everything we read in it relates to this promise and the struggle between the two seeds in one way or another. When we read the Old Testament narrative, we see that the Lord gave His people many temporary and typological fulfillments of this seed promise. A type was a person, event, or ceremony that God intended to picture some spiritual truth or aspect of the person and work of Christ. There were things that temporarily fulfilled God's promise of a deliverer, such as the judges. The judges were men and women whom the Lord raised up, anointed, and sent to deliver Israel from their oppressors. Yet they repeatedly had to deliver Israel because their deliverance was temporary. There were things that were typological—that is, that were a faint picture of the coming Savior. For example, the ark of the covenant, the tabernacle, and the temple were the dwelling places of God, foreshadowing the incarnation, for they pointed to another more perfect dwelling of God in real, living, and breathing human flesh and body (John 1:14; Col. 2:9).[6] These "incarnations" of the seed promise lifted Israel's eyes beyond this world to the world to come, yet the Seed never came during the history of the Old Testament.

Old Testament history was the up-and-down chronicle of a weak pilgrim-people who didn't have their own land. They

---

6. On this, see Daniel R. Hyde, *God in Our Midst: The Tabernacle and Our Relationship with God* (Orlando, Fla.: Reformation Trust, 2012).

were promised a land through Abraham (e.g., Gen. 12:1), given a land under Joshua (e.g., Josh. 1:2), and became a vast geopolitical nation under the reign of Solomon (1 Kings 4:21), only to become a pilgrim-people yet again, dwelling in a land not their own during the days of the prophets, such as Ezekiel. Consequently, the Jewish Old Testament scholar Nahum Sarna describes the Hebrews as "a small people in a tiny segment of the ancient world that knew independence for but brief interludes, that possessed no political power, and that generally encountered nothing but animosity."[7]

The Goal in the Prophets

The people of God, then, languished, sorrowed, and wondered. In this situation, the Old Testament prophets foresaw a climactic moment in which a young virgin woman would conceive and bear a son (Isa. 7:14). God told this people through the sermons of the prophets to look for their coming salvation with phrases such as "in that day," "in those days," "in the latter days"—what the apostle Paul called "the fullness of the time" (Gal. 4:4).

The Old Testament is replete with hope of the advent of the Lord Himself to save His people. We especially see this in the prophets, who not only spoke the word of the Lord in condemnation of the people for their disobedience but also expressed the hope, expectation, and longing of the people. For example, Isaiah cried out on behalf of the people who had become like the Lord's enemies, saying,

---

7. Nahum M. Sarna, *Understanding Genesis: The World of the Bible in the Light of History* (New York: Schocken Books, 1966), xix.

> We have become like those of old, over whom You never ruled, Those who were never called by Your name. (Isa. 63:19)

On their behalf, he invoked the Lord, calling for action:

> Oh, that You would rend the heavens!
> That You would come down!
> That the mountains might shake at Your presence!
> (Isa. 64:1; cf. Ps. 144:5)

Jeremiah also rebuked Israel's teachers for scattering God's people like bad shepherds without their sheep. Yet the Lord would regather them with caring shepherds, but most importantly by raising up a king whose name would be "THE LORD OUR RIGHTEOUSNESS" (Jer. 23:1–6). Hosea foresaw a second exodus in which the Lord would once again call His son out of Egypt (Hos. 11:1). Micah preached of a coming king who would not be ordinary; being eternal, He would cause the people to dwell securely and peacefully (Mic. 5:2–5). Israel's last prophet, Malachi, spoke of the Lord Himself coming suddenly to His temple to cleanse it, its priesthood, and its offerings (Mal. 3:1–4).

The End of the Goal

This hope of the people of God before the Lord's incarnation is also the hope of His people afterward. When the ages reached their fullness, when the time had come according to God's eternal appointment, the Seed-Son was born of the virgin Mary. The promise came true under the watchful eye of the greatest civilization the world had ever known, which had taken up residence within the promised land and "holy city" (e.g., Neh. 11:1). In the New Testament, we read these words from Paul: "We, when we were children, were in bondage under the elements of the world. But when the fullness of the time had come, God sent forth His Son, born of a woman, born under the law, to redeem those who were under the law, that we might receive the adoption as sons" (Gal. 4:3–5).

At a time of God's choosing, He put His eternal plan into action. The sovereign God sent His only Son to be born of a woman, placing Him under the same bondage in which His people were kept in order to redeem them from that bondage for God's praise. Thus, He fulfilled the promise He made millennia before in the garden of Eden. The historic Christian church has sung for generations these prophecies of the Lord's coming to save His people in the ancient advent hymn *Veni, Redemptor Gentium* composed by Ambrose of Milan (340–397):

> Savior of the nations, come,
> Virgin's Son, make here thy home!
> Marvel now, O heav'n and earth,
> That the Lord chose such a birth.[8]

This plan would be a virtual recapitulation of the history of Israel, as the Father's Son would go into Egypt (the world), die for our sins (the plagues), come out of Egypt through the Red Sea (the resurrection), lead us through the wilderness (life in this age), and bring us to Canaan (heaven). Since Christ recapitulated the history of Israel as the true Israel,

---

8. Ambrose of Milan, "Savior of the Nations Come," trans. Martin Luther (1524) and William M. Reynolds (1860), in *Trinity Psalter Hymnal* (Willow Grove, Pa.: Trinity Psalter Hymnal Joint Venture, 2018), 316.

we who in the new covenant are united to Him become like branches in the tree of the Israel of God (Rom. 9–11; Gal. 6:16). Therefore, in our Advent and Christmas celebrations, we sing of Christ and our pilgrim experience in the medieval hymn *Veni Veni Emmanuel*:

> O come, O come, Immanuel,
> And ransom captive Israel,
> That mourns in lonely exile here,
> Until the Son of God appear.
> Rejoice! Rejoice! Immanuel shall come to thee,
>   O Israel.[9]

The Climax of History

The drama of history reached its climax. There's a seamless transition from God's eternal plan to save, to the promise of that salvation in the garden (Gen. 3:15), and finally to the fulfillment of that promise in sending the Son to become flesh and dwell among us (Gal. 4:4). The Belgic Confession makes this point about the unity of God's redemptive work in Christ: "We confess, therefore, that God did fulfill the promise which he made to the fathers by the mouth of his holy prophets when he sent into the world, at the time appointed by him, his own only-begotten and eternal Son, who took upon him the form of a servant, and became like unto men" (art. 18).[10]

Two years after the Belgic Confession was written, the liturgy of the Reformed churches throughout the region of

---

9. "O Come, O Come, Emmanuel," trans. John Mason Neale, in *Trinity Psalter Hymnal*, 293.

10. Schaff, *Creeds*, 3:402. On Belgic Confession, art. 18, see Hyde, *With Heart and Mouth*, 231–43.

Germany called the Palatinate, the capital of which was Heidelberg, expressed this same truth in its "Prayer for Christmas":

> Eternal, and Almighty God, we give Thee most hearty thanks, that in Thy great love, Thou didst graciously pity us, who were doomed to eternal death for our sins, and ordained Thine only begotten Son, before the foundation of the world was laid, to be our Mediator, Atonement, and Savior; that He was promised unto our first parents in paradise, after their deplorable fall, and at the appointed time was sent into the world, that He assumed our flesh and blood, became our Brother, and in all things like unto, sin excepted. We praise Thee, that by His death He destroyed him who had the power of death, the Devil, and delivered us, who must otherwise have spent our whole life in bondage to the fear of death, from the thralldom of Satan and darkness, and translated us into the kingdom of light and eternal happiness.[11]

Incarnation

We call this event like no other the *incarnation*. Our English word comes from the Latin *incarnatio*, meaning "the act of uniting human nature with the Logos."[12] C. S. Lewis (1898–1963) called this "the central miracle asserted by Christians…. If the thing happened, it was the central event in the history of the Earth—the very thing that the whole story has been about."[13]

---

11. J. H. A. Bomberger, "The Old Palatinate Liturgy of 1563 (Continued)," *The Mercersburg Review* 2, no. 3 (May 1850): 275.

12. Muller, *Dictionary of Latin and Greek Theological Terms*, 152.

13. C. S. Lewis, *Miracles* (1947; repr., San Francisco: Harper Collins, 2001), 173, 174.

The New Testament says the incarnation was the event when "God sent forth His Son" (Gal. 4:4) to be "conceived…of [by] the Holy Spirit" (Matt. 1:20; see also Luke 1:35) and "born of a woman" (Gal. 4:4); when "the Word [Logos] became flesh" (John 1:14); and when "God was manifested in the flesh" (1 Tim. 3:16). This was the event that the prophets and angels were so desirous of understanding (1 Peter 1:10–12) and so privileged to announce. The angel heralded this event, saying, "And they shall call His name Immanuel, which is translated, 'God with us'" (Matt. 1:23).

Conception

The incarnation, then, is that act and event of God in which His eternal Son was conceived and born as a human child. Yet we so often speak of the "virgin birth" that we forget the "virgin conception." Both make up the incarnation. Before we can speak of the Son being born, we speak of His conception in the womb of Mary. Michael Horton so remarkably states, "God became a zygote in the uterus of a Jewish virgin who was pledged to be married to Joseph."[14] This is the amazing truth that our forefathers in the ancient church stretched human language to explain in the face of many heresies.[15] As Christians, we believe there is one God who exists in three persons. One

---

14. Michael Horton, *We Believe: Recovering the Essentials of the Apostles' Creed* (Nashville: Word, 1998), 76.

15. The word "heresy" comes from the Greek word *hairesis*, which is used to describe dissensions and factions (1 Cor. 11:19; Gal. 5:20) as well as "destructive heresies" (2 Peter 2:1)—that is, destructive opinions or teachings. In the early church, "heresy" meant false teaching against the accepted faith of the churches (e.g., Justin Martyr, *Dialog with Trypho the Jew*, chap. 35).

of those persons, the Son of God, added to Himself humanity. Thus, John simply says, "the Word became flesh" (John 1:14).

This dramatic and climactic event, whether we speak of it theologically as the incarnation and nativity or popularly as Christmas, seems to have lost its significance today. It is something that has become so mundane, so banal that the unbelieving culture lets "Christmas" roll off its tongue all too easily. The incarnation, however, is no mere phrase; it was a climactic, redemptive event. It was a moment in which there was hushed silence in heaven and earth as God did something He had never done before—and it was followed by exuberant praise: "Come, behold the works of the LORD" (Ps. 46:8). What we need is not simply to define this term in an annual Christmas sermon, as if the incarnation were simply a vocabulary lesson or a doctrine to pull off the shelf when required; instead, we need to understand its significance so we can apply its benefits to our ongoing worship, spirituality, church, and family life.

The Giving of the Father

Lest we turn this mystery into triviality, remember that Scripture says God the Father has only one Son. As we read in the account of Christ's baptism, the Father spoke from heaven, saying, "You are My beloved Son; in You I am well pleased" (Luke 3:22). Notice the present tense verb "You *are*." The Father didn't use a past tense verb, "*were*," as if the Son was God but ceased to be God on earth. He didn't use a perfect tense, "*have become*," as if this sonship didn't begin until Jesus's baptism. He didn't use a future tense, "*will be*," as if this sonship would be given in the future. No, He used a present tense, "*are*," because

He is "the eternal natural Son of God" the Father (Heidelberg Catechism 33).[16] Jesus alludes to His eternal relationship with the Father in His High Priestly Prayer: "And now, O Father, glorify Me together with Yourself, with the glory which I had with You before the world was" (John 17:5). Thus, the incarnation happened when God the Father "at the appointed time" sent His only beloved Son out of His glorious presence, giving His dear Son to His people on earth: "For God so loved the world that He gave His only begotten Son" (John 3:16). What a great sacrifice this was on the part of the Father!

The Emptying of the Son

It was also a great sacrifice on the part of the Son. The sacrifice was not that there was something bad about becoming a man; after all, God created man in His image (Gen. 1:26–27) and declared him "very good" (Gen. 1:31); man also in some sense remains an image bearer of God (Gen. 9:6; James 3:9). The sacrifice of the Son was undergoing a humiliation by identifying Himself with fallen men and women like us in the incarnation, but especially on the cross. Notice how Paul describes this in Philippians 2:5–8: "Christ Jesus...being in the form of God, did not consider it robbery to be equal with God, but made Himself of no reputation, taking the form of a bondservant, and coming in the likeness of men. And being found in appearance as a man, He humbled Himself and became obedient to the point of death, even the death of the cross."

What Paul says about the death of Jesus Christ presupposes the incarnation. As God ("being in the form of God"),

---

16. Schaff, *Creeds*, 3:318.

Jesus Christ did not regard His equality with God as *harpagmos*. This Greek word, translated as "robbery" in Philippians 2, is something that a person already has and is using for himself. Thus, Jesus did not regard His equality with God as something to use for His own advantage, but for the advantage of others. Instead of using His equality with God for His welfare, Jesus, says Paul, "made Himself of no reputation"—that is, He literally emptied Himself by pouring out Himself in death as a man. This emptying was the result of taking on Himself the form of a servant, the likeness of men and the fashion of men.[17]

The eternal Son underwent self-denial, leaving His heavenly glory with the Father in the fellowship of the Holy Spirit to unite Himself to fallen people and to die for them on the cross as an accursed sinner (2 Cor. 5:21; Gal. 3:13). Is this an insignificant doctrine? Is incarnation just some ordinary word? It's not ordinary for the pilgrim people of God, or for the Son who became incarnate, or for the Father who sent His Son.

But didn't the Son cease to be God when He became a man? Doesn't Paul say He "emptied Himself" (Phil. 2:7 NASB)? It's true that there are theologians who teach that God the Son laid aside His divine nature while on earth or that He divested himself of His divine attributes or prerogatives of His deity. They teach this based on the Greek word *kenōsis*, translated

---

17. On Philippians 2:6–8, see Hywel R. Jones, *Philippians* (Ross-shire, Scotland: Christian Focus, 1993), 67–78; F. F. Bruce, *Philippians*, New International Biblical Commentary (Peabody, Mass.: Hendrickson, 1983, 1989), 68–72; John Owen, *Meditations and Discourses on the Glory of Christ*, in *The Works of John Owen*, ed. William H. Goold (1850–1853; repr., Edinburgh: Banner of Truth, 1965), 1:323–33.

"made of no reputation" or "emptied." Yet this can't be true since God is immutable; that is, He doesn't change (Mal. 3:6). What does it mean, then, that the Son emptied Himself? What Paul is saying is that the Son, who before the incarnation was "in the form of God," was of the same essence as the Father, being invisible and spiritual. After the incarnation, He took the "form of a bondservant, and [came] in the likeness of men." Thus, the eternal Son was humbled to the point of the death of the cross. In the incarnation, "Christ added to himself that which he was not; he did not lose what he was."[18] John Owen (1616–1683) said, "The Son of God becoming in time to be what he was not, the Son of man, ceased not thereby to be what he was, even the eternal Son of God."[19] This stooping down from eternity into time, from immortality into mortality, from immutability into mutability, was the Son's humiliation, emptying, and becoming without reputation.

A Wonder
The incarnation of Christ is the wonder and mystery we're attempting to grasp. The great wonder of this self-denial of the Father and the Son is that it's for our benefit. The Nicene Creed beautifully proclaims the wonder of the incarnation and its benefit when we confess our belief in the Lord Jesus Christ, who is "the only-begotten Son of God, begotten of the Father before all worlds, [God of God], Light of Light, very God of very God; begotten, not made, being of one substance [essence] with the Father; by whom all things were made."

---

18. Augustine, as quoted in Berkouwer, *Person of Christ*, 94.
19. Owen, *Meditations and Discourses on the Glory of Christ*, in *Works*, 1:326.

The Creed thus summarizes the wonder of the incarnation: the "Son of God...for us men and for our salvation, came down from heaven and was incarnate by the Holy Ghost of the Virgin Mary, and was made man."[20]

In the Nicene Creed, we not only confess with our mouths but believe in our hearts the marvelous wonder that God became man. It's important for us to recapture a glimpse of this mystery because we all too often view either the death or resurrection of Jesus Christ as the high point of redemptive history. The incarnation was the wonder of wonders in that it began the string of events we call the work of Christ. The apostle Paul said, "If Christ is not risen, then our preaching is empty [vain] and your faith is also empty [vain].... You are still in your sins!" (1 Cor. 15:14, 17). In a similar manner, we can say that if the Son of God isn't incarnate, then our preaching and our faith are in vain while at the same time we're still in our sins. Without the incarnation there's no purpose to or power in the life, death, and resurrection of Christ. In the aforementioned words of Warfield, "The Incarnation is the hinge on which the Christian system turns.... No Incarnation, no Christianity in any distinctive sense."[21]

We must recapture this "mystery of godliness" (1 Tim. 3:16) in our preaching, worship, and community life, being filled with amazement and reverence that "He who was without a mother in heaven was without a father on earth."[22] This

---

20. See Appendix 1: The Ecumenical Creeds.
21. Warfield, "'Two Natures,'" 106.
22. J. Van Bruggen, *The Church Says Amen: An Exposition of the Belgic Confession*, trans. Johanna VanderPlas (Neerlandia, Alta., Canada: Inheritance, 2003), 106.

wonder of the incarnation was expressed by one of the ancient fathers, Gregory of Nazianzus (325–389). Echoing the Nicene Creed, he said,

> The Word of God Himself, Who is before all worlds, the Invisible, the Incomprehensible, the Bodiless, the Beginning of beginning, the Light of Light, the Source of Life and Immortality, the Image of the Archetype, the Immovable Seal, the Unchangeable Image, the Father's Definition and Word, came to His own Image, and took on Him Flesh for the sake of our flesh, and mingled Himself with an intelligent soul for my soul's sake, purifying like by like; and in all points except sin was made Man.

Note the importance of all this: "for the sake of our flesh… for my soul's sake." The Son didn't become incarnate for Himself but for us—for me! Continuing, Nazianzus said:

> He came forth then, as God, with That which He had assumed; one Person in two natures…. O new commingling; O strange conjunction! the Self-existent comes into Being, the Uncreated is created, That which cannot be contained is contained…. And He who gives riches becomes poor; for He assumes the poverty of my flesh, that I may assume the riches of His Godhead. He that is full empties Himself; for He empties Himself of His Glory for a short while, that I may have a share in His Fulness.[23]

---

23. Gregory of Nazianzus, "The Second Oration on Easter" 45.9, in *Nicene and Post-Nicene Fathers*, Second Series, ed. Philip Schaff and Henry Wace (1894; repr., Peabody, Mass.: Hendrickson, 2004), 7:425–26.

Since the incarnation is such a wonderful truth, we must take up the call of the psalmist to "behold the works of the LORD" (Ps. 46:8), stretching our imaginations in light of this event, meditating on the reason for it, and praying for God the Holy Spirit to apply it to our hearts and lives.

A Trinitarian Work

The incarnation is also a wonder to believe and confess because it's the work of our glorious and gracious triune God—Father, Son, and Holy Spirit. While the Son assumed a human nature (Ps. 40:6; Heb. 10:5), the Father sent His Son (Gal. 4:4) and formed that nature, overshadowing the virgin Mary (Luke 1:35) and doing so by the ineffable work of the Holy Spirit (Matt. 1:20). This is important because the one God who exists in three distinct persons has one will for us and for our salvation. His will is executed in a harmonious way as the Father sets the stage, the Son performs the work, and the Holy Spirit directs the work to its goal and climax in the incarnation.

This work of our triune God in the incarnation is vital to our witness to the world. Think, for example, about how immense the love of God the Father is for His fallen world. Remembering how God sent His Son to become man by the work of the Holy Spirit should affect our witnessing to agnostics. When witnessing to Muslims, who overemphasize the sovereignty and infinity of Allah as God, we should remember the personal, intimate nature of God, who relates to us on our own level by becoming one of us. Think about the possibilities that the traditional theology of the incarnation speaks to a multicultural society. God the Father loves the world.

This is evidenced in the Son of God becoming a man—an ethnic Jew who sought the Gentiles in order to incorporate both into His kingdom.

The incarnation, then, was that wonderful event for the benefit of a fallen race that was the goal and climax of human history, in which a loving Father sent His eternal Son into the world to become a man through the powerful and mysterious working of the Holy Spirit. The incarnation draws sinners into the fellowship of the Father's eternal and heavenly life as His sons and daughters in the Son within the communion and fellowship of the Holy Spirit.

> Our little Lord, we give thee praise
> That thou has deigned to take our ways.
> Born of a maid a man to be,
> And all the angels sing to thee.
>
> The eternal Father's Son he lay
> Cradled in a crib of hay.
> The everlasting God appears
> In our frail flesh and blood and tears.
>
> What the globe could not enwrap
> Nestled lies in Mary's lap.
> Just a baby, very wee,
> Yet the Lord of all the world is he.[24]

---

24. A children's Christmas carol by Martin Luther as quoted in Roland H. Bainton, *Here I Stand: A Life of Martin Luther* (New York: Abingdon Press, 1950), 303–4.

TWO

The God Who Is Also Man: Christ's Two Natures

> I could wish that I myself were accursed from Christ for my brethren, my countrymen according to the flesh… of whom are the fathers and from whom, according to the flesh, Christ came, who is over all, the eternally blessed God. Amen.
>
> —ROMANS 9:3–5

The great story of the Bible is that the eternal Son of God came from heaven to earth and became a man in order to take man from earth to heaven.[1] I hope you're thinking, *What does this really mean?* Does this mean the Son ceased to be God during His earthly life, then became God again at the resurrection and His ascension into heaven? Does this mean the Son absorbed a man's body, turning Himself into a superman—some sort of Greek or Roman mythological divine being? In this chapter we'll delve into these kinds of questions. What we'll see is that the clear yet ever mysterious teaching of the Holy Scripture is that the Lord and Savior

---

1. Athanasius, *On the Incarnation of the Word*, in *Nicene and Post-Nicene Fathers*, Second Series, ed. Archibald Robertson (1892; repr., Peabody, Mass.: Hendrickson, 2004), 4:65.

Jesus Christ was and is *both* God and man. Johannes Wollebius (1589–1629) wrote that in being both God and man, the Son "remained what he was, and was made what he had not been."[2] Regarding the Son becoming what He wasn't before (that is, human), Irenaeus (130–202) said, "The Word of God was made man, and He who was the Son of God became the Son of man, that man, having been taken into the Word, and receiving the adoption, might become the son of God."[3]

Defining Terms

Since it's always necessary for people to communicate well so that they understand and don't "talk past" each other, it's important to define some key terminology I'll be using.

Nature

In the previous chapter, I explained that Christ has two natures—divine and human. It's necessary to understand what this means. A "nature" is something that has its own peculiar qualities, attributes, and characteristics.[4] Simply, a nature is what makes a thing a thing. The nature of water is that it's made of two molecules of hydrogen and one molecule of oxygen. This is its unique characteristic. We use the term "nature" in reference to the incarnation because being God and being

---

2. Johannes Wollebius, *Compendium Theologiae Christianae*, in *Reformed Dogmatics: J. Wollebius, G. Voetius [and] F. Turretin*, ed. John W. Beardslee (1965; repr., Grand Rapids: Baker Book House, 1977), 87.

3. Irenaeus, *Against Heresies* 3.19, in *Ante-Nicene Fathers*, ed. Alexander Roberts and James Donaldson (1885; repr., Peabody, Mass.: Hendrickson, 2004), 1:448, col. 2.

4. M. J. Bosma, *Exposition of Reformed Doctrine*, 4th ed. (Grand Rapids: Smitter Book Company, 1927), 139–40; cf. Berkhof, *Systematic Theology*, 321.

man are two different things. Being God means one thing, and being man means another; they each have their own nature with peculiar qualities, attributes, and characteristics. For example, Christ's divine nature is eternal while His human nature is temporal. His divine nature is infinite while His human nature is finite. These are peculiar qualities, attributes, and characteristics of each nature. The Belgic Confession simply sums up this issue when it says, "We believe that by this conception the person of the Son is inseparably united and connected with the human nature; so that there are not two Sons of God, nor two persons, but two natures united in one single person; yet each nature retains its own distinct properties" (art. 19).[5]

The Confession can say this because eternality and infinity are qualities of the nature of God, while temporality and finitude are attributes of human nature. Jesus Christ has both; therefore, He has two natures.

Person

The traditional theological term we use in reference to the mysterious teaching of how the Lord's divine and human natures relate is "hypostatic union." The word "hypostatic" comes from the Greek word *hupostasis*, which is translated as "person." What do I mean when I speak of the person of Christ? Simply, "a person is a nature with something added, namely, independent subsistence; individuality."[6] When we

---

5. Schaff, *Creeds*, 3:404. On Belgic Confession, art. 19, see Hyde, *With Heart and Mouth*, 245–57.

6. Berkhof, *Systematic Theology*, 321. Bosma makes this a little more confusing than it ought to be when he writes of a person as anything "having

speak of humans as persons, we mean that they are living, intelligent people who have the ability to exercise a will separately from another person. When we speak of the hypostatic union, we are trying to communicate that there was and is a joining of the divine and human natures in the person (*hupostasis*) of Christ. Thus, in the one person of Christ are united two natures—the divine and the human, God and man.

At this point we can stop and acknowledge with awe the mystery of this doctrine. Which of us finite sinners can understand what this union of two into one is like? We can take comfort and gain confidence that Jesus Christ is the Savior of the world precisely because He's complex and mysterious, being both God and man, the Creator and the creature, while we are simply human and creatures. If He were merely like us, He would not be worthy of the titles God and Lord.

Theology by Negation

Because this union of the Lord's natures in His person is mysterious, we can't fully describe it positively in human language. Therefore, one of the ways we apprehend this mystery is to say what it's not in order to say what it is. This is what the ancient Christian theologians called *via negativa* theology or *apophatic* theology, which is doing theology by way of negation. For example, we speak of God being *in*visible because we can't see Him; *im*mutable because He doesn't change. This way of expressing the person of Christ in two natures is pertinent because the hypostatic union is "a mystery which defies

---

life, intelligence, will and a separate existence." The reason this is confusing is because Christ has two wills—a divine and a human will. A will is of the nature of being God and man. *Exposition of Reformed Doctrine*, 140.

explanation."[7] Here's how Wollebius applied this ancient practice of negation to the union of the two natures in the person of Christ. Notice the negativity:

> It is *not* a union of essence, like the unity of the divine persons.
>
> It is *not* a union of essence and power, in which sense the essence of Christ is present in all things.
>
> It is *not* merely the presence of grace.
>
> It is *not* a natural union, such as that of power and matter.
>
> It is *not* a matter of relation, like that of a friend with friend.
>
> It is *not* mystical, like the presence of Christ in the faithful.
>
> It is *not* sacramental, like the presence in the holy supper,
>
> but it is hypostatic or personal;
>
> that is, to explain more fully, so as to avoid the Eutychian and Nestorian heresies, it is
>
> (1) *without* change of the divine person,
>
> (2) *without* separation of the natures, contrary to the teaching of the Nestorians,
>
> (3) *without* confusion of the natures, contrary to the teachings of the Eutychians, and
>
> (4) *without* separation.[8]

---

7. Berkhof, *Systematic Theology*, 321.

8. Wollebius, *Compendium Theologiae Christianae*, 91; cf. Donald G. Bloesch, *Jesus Christ: Savior and Lord*, Christian Foundations (Downers Grove, Ill.: InterVarsity Press, 1997), 56.

After listing in seven ways what the union between Christ's divine and human natures isn't, Wollebius positively stated that it was "hypostatic or personal." He went on to explain this with four more negative assertions. Such is the mystery of our Lord. This is alright. We're treading holy ground here in the wilderness.

Confusion of the Two Natures

Wollebius's explanation may sound good and right to us, yet this confession of Christ having two natures was challenged throughout the history of the church. When we confess that Christ has two natures, we're agreeing with the "catholic consensus."[9]

> The Word of God Himself, Who is before all worlds, the Invisible, the Incomprehensible, the Bodiless, the Beginning of beginning, the Light of Light, the Source of Life and Immortality, the Image of the Archetype, the Immovable Seal, the Unchangeable Image, the Father's Definition and Word, came to His own Image, and took on Him Flesh for the sake of our flesh, and mingled Himself with an intelligent soul for my soul's sake, purifying like by like; and in all points except sin was made Man.

Praxeas

As early as 208, the North African theologian Tertullian (155–240) wrote against Praxeas. In trying to keep the unity of God,

---

9. This simply means the universal acceptance across all times in the church and in all places of this teaching. This does not mean this is a Roman Catholic doctrine; rather, it is a Christian doctrine. Cf. Berkhof, *Systematic Theology*, 316.

Praxeas said that Jesus was a man and Christ was the father. As Tertullian pointed out, this led to the teaching that Jesus Christ was neither man nor God but a third thing (*tertium quid*). He began his refutation by asserting the following: "The Word, therefore, is incarnate; and this must be the point of our inquiry: How the Word became flesh,—whether it was by having been transfigured, as it were, in the flesh, or by having really clothed Himself in flesh. Certainly it was by a real clothing of Himself in flesh."[10] He went on to state that Christians believed this because God is unchangeable:

> For...we...believe God to be unchangeable, and incapable of form, as being eternal. But transfiguration is the destruction of that which previously existed. For whatsoever is transfigured into some other thing ceases to be that which it had been, and begins to be that which it previously was not. God, however, neither ceases to be what He was, nor can He be any other thing than what He is. The Word is God, and "the Word of the Lord remaineth for ever,"—even by holding on unchangeably in His own proper form. Now, if He admits not of being transfigured, it must follow that He be understood in this sense to have become flesh, when He comes to be in the flesh, and is manifested, and is seen, and is handled by means of the flesh; since all the other points likewise require to be thus understood. For if the Word became flesh by a transfiguration and change of substance, it follows at once that Jesus must be a substance compounded of two substances—of flesh and spirit,—a

---

10. Tertullian, *Against Praxeas*, in *Ante-Nicene Fathers*, ed. A. Cleveland Coxe (1885; repr., Peabody, Mass.: Hendrickson, 2004), 3:623.

kind of mixture, like *electrum*, composed of gold and silver; and it begins to be neither gold (that is to say, spirit) nor silver (that is to say, flesh),—the one being changed by the other, and a third substance produced.

According to Tertullian, the result of confusing the two natures in the person of the incarnate Son is that He would have "ceased to be the Word, which was made flesh; nor can He be Man incarnate for He is not properly flesh, and it was flesh, which the Word became. Being compounded, therefore, of both, He actually is neither; He is rather some third substance, very different from either."[11]

Eutyches

In the mid-fifth century, the proponents of what would later be called Eutychianism, though, were the most vehement advocates of this error of confusing the two distinct natures. Eutyches (378–454), the namesake of this teaching, was the leader of a monastery of three hundred monks outside the

---

11. Tertullian, *Against Praxeas*, in *Ante-Nicene Fathers*, 3:624. He went on to state the orthodox doctrine against Praxeas:

> But the truth is, we find that He is expressly set forth as both God and Man…certainly in all respects as the Son of God and the Son of Man, being God and Man, differing no doubt according to each substance in its own especial property, inasmuch as the Word is nothing else but God, and the flesh nothing else but Man…. We see plainly the twofold state, which is not confounded, but conjoined in One Person—Jesus, God and Man…. The property of each nature is so wholly preserved, that the Spirit on the one hand did all things in Jesus suitable to Itself, such as miracles, and mighty deeds, and wonders; and the Flesh, on the other hand, exhibited the affections which belong to it. It was hungry under the devil's temptation, thirsty with the Samaritan woman, wept over Lazarus, was troubled even unto death, and at last actually died.

great imperial city of Constantinople. His teaching so overemphasized the divine nature of Christ that it inevitably made Christ to be one person with one nature. He taught that the eternal Son of God either absorbed a human nature at the incarnation or that these two natures fused into a "third thing" (*tertium quid*).

Monophysites

Later in church history, those who held this point of view made their theology more concise and came to be known as the Monophysites, for they confessed Christ to have one (*mono*) nature (*phusis*). The Monophysites divided into several different sects: the Theopaschites, the Phthartolatrists, and the Arphthartodocetists. The Theopaschites believed that God suffered on the cross. The Phthartolatrists believed that Christ had a human nature like ours and therefore worshiped Him as a corruptible person. The Arphthartodocetists believed that Christ's human nature was not like ours but rather was endowed with divine properties such as imperishability and incorruptibility.

Orthodox Response

In essence, Praxeas, the Eutychians, and the Monophysites taught that Christ's divine nature was like hot water and His human nature was like cold water that combined to make a third kind of water: warm. Orthodox Christian theologians, during and after the time of Eutyches, rejected this idea that Jesus Christ was a "third thing." They claimed it made Christ neither truly God nor truly man. His divinity absorbed humanity and made both divinity and humanity different from before. Eutyches's teaching was a serious heresy, a false teaching against the Christian faith. If Jesus's humanity became divine, He wasn't of one substance (*homoousian*) with our humanity; thus, Jesus wouldn't be a human like we are. As we'll see later, if He's not human, He can't be our Redeemer from the guilt and corruption of sin. A true human who lived a perfect life and died a sacrificial death in our place was necessary to satisfy God's wrath for our sins. If Jesus was neither true God nor true man, He wasn't our Savior. Flavian, bishop of Constantinople, condemned and deposed Eutyches from office. As a result, great turmoil ensued throughout the ancient world. The result was that in 449, Eutyches's followers convened for what has come to be known as the Robber Council, for they condemned Flavian and reinstated Eutyches.[12]

During this time Leo I (400–461), the bishop of Rome, wrote a response to the teaching of Eutyches in a letter to Flavian known as the Tome. This letter became an influential piece of the fourth ecumenical Council of Chalcedon (451), which condemned Eutyches. Leo's Tome made five important points:

1) Jesus Christ has two distinct natures.

2) These two natures are united in one person with each performing its proper function [the human nature did human things like eat; the divine nature did divine things like uphold the universe].

3) From this unity of person follows a *verbal* communication of attributes:

---

12. For a summary of this history, see David Christie-Murray, *A History of Heresy* (Oxford: Oxford University Press, 1976), 69–83.

> a) The properties of both natures may be attributed to the person (e.g., we can say the person of Christ is omniscient because of the divine nature but also limited in knowledge because of the humanity).
>
> b) The suffering of the God-man can be regarded as an infinite suffering, because it was God on the cross, although the divine nature is impassible (incapable of suffering).
>
> 4) The work of redemption required a Mediator who was divine and human, passible (capable of suffering) and impassible, mortal and immortal; yet the humanity did not detract from the divinity.
>
> 5) The humanity of Christ is permanent; to deny this is Docetism.[13]

As historic Protestants, we confess with the church catholic that although the Son of God "inseparably united" Himself to a human nature, nevertheless "each nature retains its own distinct properties" (Belgic Confession, art. 19).[14] He didn't absorb or change a human nature but assumed one. As the Athanasian Creed says, Christ is "one, not by conversion of the Godhead into flesh, but by taking of the manhood into God. One altogether, not by confusion of substance, but by unity of person" (§§35–36). The Definition of the Council of Chalcedon (451) rejected Eutyches's doctrine when it said that the Son, our Lord Jesus Christ, is "to be acknowledged in two natures, inconfusedly, unchangeably…the distinction of the natures being by no means taken away by the union,

---

13. Adapted from Berkhof, *History of Christian Doctrines*, 106–7.
14. Schaff, *Creeds*, 3:404.

but rather the property of each nature being preserved, and concurring in one Person and Subsistence."[15]

This discussion illuminates for us the importance of being truly catholic in our faith and life as Christians and Christian communities. Our confession of the great creeds of the ancient churches says to the communities around us that our faith and life as local congregations aren't novel, the result of religious whims, or contrived to control people with religion. Instead, our faith is transcendent and meaningful to every age and race of humanity. This is particularly important in an age that is antiauthoritarian and searching for transcendent reality. The creeds root our authority not in the personality and charisma of the pastor but in the Scriptures as historically confessed; as well, they root our faith and experience in that which is real and historical, not just in a passing fad or feeling.

Rejection of the Two Natures

Even worse than the doctrine of Eutyches was that of Docetism. This was a teaching in the early period of the church that Jesus only appeared to be human. His humanity was a phantom of what He really was—a divine being. The term "Docetism" comes from the Greek word *dokein*, which means "to seem; to appear." This is also the doctrine of the modern-day religion Christian Science.[16] This teaching found its roots in Greek philosophy, which said that matter was inherently evil but that spirit was good. The result was the belief that the

---

15. Schaff, *Creeds*, 2:62.
16. Mary Baker Eddy, *Science and Health with the Key to the Scriptures* (1875; repr., Boston: First Church of Christ Scientist, 1934).

divine couldn't become what was inherently evil and unbecoming of his divinity. Yet the New Testament refutes this false doctrine in places such as 1 John, which describes the reality of our Lord's divinity as well as His humanity. In the first chapter, John said he wrote the following in order that his readers' "joy may be full" (v. 4):

> That which was from the beginning, which *we have heard*, which *we have seen with our eyes*, which *we have looked upon*, and *our hands have handled*, concerning the Word of life—the life was *manifested*, and *we have seen*, and bear witness, and declare to you that eternal life which was with the Father and was *manifested* to us—that which *we have seen and heard* we declare to you, that you also may have fellowship with us; and truly our fellowship is with the Father and with His Son Jesus Christ. (1 John 1:1–3)

The reality and tangibility of the Son of God in human flesh was the basis on which John could write about the reality and tangibility of our joy in Christ. Without the incarnation, there would be no reason for ultimate joy. Several chapters later, John wrote:

> By this you know the Spirit of God: Every spirit that confesses that Jesus Christ *has come in the flesh* is of God, and every spirit that does not confess that Jesus Christ *has come in the flesh* is not of God. And this is the spirit of the Antichrist, which you have heard was coming, and is now already in the world....
>
> In this the love of God was manifested toward us, that God has sent His only begotten Son *into the world*, that we might live through Him. (4:2–3, 9)

The one great test of a true or false prophet, according to John, is whether he confesses the reality of the incarnation and not merely an appearance of an incarnation. He who confesses the reality of the Son in the flesh is of God, and he who doesn't is an antichrist.

The early church fathers also rejected this teaching as false doctrine. Ignatius of Antioch (30–107) offered up one such rejection:

> Stop your ears, therefore, when any one speaks to you at variance with Jesus Christ, who was descended from David, and was also of Mary; who was truly born, and did eat and drink. He was truly persecuted under Pontius Pilate; He was truly crucified, and [truly] died, in the sight of beings in heaven, and on earth, and under the earth. He was also truly raised from the dead, His Father quickening Him, even as after the same manner His Father will so raise up us who believe in Him by Christ Jesus, apart from whom we do not possess the true life. *But* if, as *some* that are without God, that is, the unbelieving, *say, that He only seemed to suffer* (they themselves only seeming to exist), then why am I in bonds?[17]

Application

What does this classic doctrine of the two natures of Christ mean in a pluralistic society? Put another way, should we be politically correct and forget about classic theological distinctions for the sake of peace and unity? We can imagine a

---

17. *The Epistle of Ignatius to the Trallians*, chaps. 9–10, in *Ante-Nicene Fathers*, ed. Alexander Roberts and James Donaldson (1885; repr., Peabody, Mass.: Hendrickson, 2004), 1:69–70.

person saying, "After all, don't the Monophysite Christians [the Coptic church] in Egypt, Iraq, and other parts of the Middle East love the Lord?" While we need to be charitable and recognize that it's not the doctrine of Christ that saves but Christ Himself, we also need to say strongly that a person can't really love the Lord who doesn't truly know Him. Jesus is who He is, and for us to love Him as we think He is, is not to love Him but to love someone we've created in our minds—which is to love ourselves. It is essential for us to be precise in our theological language, since "theology" means, after all, "words about God." We need to talk about God as God has revealed that we should. The Son has two natures because only God can save humans from their sin, and we need a Savior who is both God and man at the same time.

As we've seen so far, our blessed triune God sent the eternal Son to earth. He was and is both true and fully God and true and fully human. He has two distinct natures, which can't be confused or denied but must be believed and adored by faith. It's to these natures of the person of Christ that we'll turn one by one to see just how divine and human He really was—and remains.

> Beautiful Savior! King of creation!
> Son of God and Son of Man!
> Truly I'd love Thee, truly I'd serve Thee,
> Light of my soul, my joy, my crown.[18]

---

18. "Beautiful Savior," trans. J. A. Seiss, in *Psalter Hymnal* (Grand Rapids: Christian Reformed Church, 1976), #373.

THREE

The Son of God: Christ's Divine Nature

> Then He said to Thomas, "Reach your finger here, and look at My hands; and reach your hand here, and put it into My side. Do not be unbelieving, but believing."
> And Thomas answered and said to Him, "My Lord and my God!"
> —JOHN 20:27–28

The high point of human history and the history of God's plan of redemption as revealed in Scripture is the incarnation. The doctrine of the incarnation teaches us that the eternal Son of God entered temporal time, the infinite Son entered the finiteness of space, and the transcendent Son entered our immanent history—all to become a human being. Because of this He has both a divine and a human nature, retaining what He was as divine while assuming what He was not as human. In this chapter and the next we want to explore and meditate on what the Scriptures say about each of these two natures individually.

The Deity of the Son: A Fundamental Doctrine

The deity of our Lord Jesus Christ is a fundamental truth proclaimed by historic Christianity. In the words of the Apostles'

The Son of God: Christ's Divine Nature

Creed, Jesus Christ is the Father's "only begotten Son." The foundational nature of this doctrine is such that even in our day, when seeker-sensitive and culturally accommodated churches are innumerable and much of the professing church lacks doctrinal knowledge,[1] most churches confess the deity of Jesus Christ in their statements of faith. For example, the ever-popular Joel Osteen Ministries states, "We believe in one God who exists in three distinct persons: Father, Son, and Holy Spirit.... We believe Jesus Christ is the Son of God who came to this earth as Savior of the world."[2] The flagship of the modern seeker-sensitive church movement, Willow Creek Community Church (South Barrington, Illinois), states, "We believe there is one true, holy God, eternally existing in three equal persons—Father, Son, and Holy Spirit."[3]

In examining the biblical data concerning the Lord's divinity, I want to approach this issue from a redemptive-historical point of view. This means I don't want to simplistically rely on proof texts of the Bible, with a verse here or there about Jesus being God. Instead, I want to trace how this doctrine progressively unfolds throughout the Scriptures from Genesis through Revelation. In doing this, I confess with the ancient theologian of Alexandria, Origen (185–254), that "it is impossible to commit to writing all those particulars

---

1. For example, see the biannual "State of Theology" survey: https://thestateoftheology.com.
2. "The Trinity," About Lakewood, Lakewood Church.com, https://www.lakewoodchurch.com/about.
3. "Beliefs and Values," About, WillowCreek.org, https://www.willowcreek.org/en/about/beliefs-and-values.

which belong to the glory of the Saviour."[4] Knowing this, we see that a redemptive-historical method is advantageous. We have a unique vantage point, living after Jesus's resurrection and having received the fullness of the Spirit's gifts to the church (Acts 2; 1 Corinthians 12; Ephesians 4). In fact, the apostle Peter says that the salvation proclaimed to us in the preached word about "the sufferings of Christ and the glories that would follow" (1 Peter 1:11) are what the prophets "inquired and searched carefully" to understand. It's also what the angels "desire to look into" (vv. 10, 12). It's interesting that the verb Peter uses of the angels, "to look into" (*parakupsai*), is the same that John used of himself and Peter "stooping down" (*parakupsas*) to look into the tomb (John 20:5).[5] As new covenant believers, we have in Jesus He whom the ancient prophets and angelic armies longed to know.

His Deity in the Old Testament

And God Said

The Scriptures open with the grand declaration, "In the beginning God created the heavens and the earth" (Gen. 1:1). Then God brought order to the earth in six days with the recurring refrain, "Then God said" (vv. 3, 6, 9, 11, 14, 20, 24, 26). Creation came into being through the powerful word of God. When He spoke, things were. The psalmist reflected

---

4. Origen, *De Principiis* 2.6.1, in *Ante-Nicene* Fathers, ed. Alexander Roberts and James Donaldson, rev. A. Cleveland Coxe, trans. Frederick Crombie (1885; repr., Peabody, Mass.: Hendrickson, 2004), 4:281.

5. Peter uses the aorist active infinite form while John uses the aorist active participle form of *parakuptō*.

this creation narrative: "By the word of the LORD the heavens were made" (Ps. 33:6).

We need to note how the New Testament apostles interpreted these words of Genesis 1. They teach that God the Father made everything through His Son, our Lord Jesus. The opening of John's gospel is the narrative of a new creation. Note how these creations parallel each other:

The First Creation (Genesis 1:1–4)	**The New Creation (John 1:1–5)**
¹In the beginning God created the heavens and the earth. ²The earth was without form, and void; and darkness was on the face of the deep. And the Spirit of God was hovering over the face of the waters. ³Then God said, "Let there be light"; and there was light. ⁴And God saw the light, that it was good; and God divided the light from the darkness.	¹In the beginning was the Word, and the Word was with God, and the Word was God. ²He was in the beginning with God. ³All things were made through Him, and without Him nothing was made that was made. ⁴In Him was life, and the life was the light of men. ⁵And the light shines in the darkness, and the darkness did not comprehend it.

In his gospel, John goes beyond "the beginning" (*bere'shit*), which in Genesis 1:1 speaks of the beginning of time and all that is. The "beginning" (*archē*) of which he writes in John 1:1 is "the absolute starting-point" of eternity.[6] John gives us a way

---

6. D. A. Carson, *The Gospel according to John* (Grand Rapids: Eerdmans, 1991), 113. See also Raymond E. Brown, *The Gospel according to John*

of understanding the eternal relationship that existed between the Word (*Logos*), who is the Son, and God, who is the Father. The striking thing John says is that from eternity the Word existed; He "was" (*ēn*). Thus He was "with God" (*pros ton theon*) and "was God" (*theos ēn*; John 1:1).

John then refers to the first creation, saying, "All things were made through Him"—that is, the Word—and "without Him nothing was made that was made" (John 1:3). Genesis 1 records that God spoke the world into being. John says that the word of God, in some mysterious way, was the eternal Word. The "disciple whom Jesus loved" (John 21:20) could say explicitly in his gospel what Moses could only record as fact. Moses didn't understand the full revelation of God as triune, yet we on this side of the resurrection of Christ can comprehend His work at creation. Several other New Testament writers explain the creation narrative in the same way. We read in creedal-like fashion of the Son's participation in the divine work of creation. The apostles teach that God the Father created the world and all things "by" or "through" His Son, Jesus Christ (1 Cor. 8:6; Col. 1:16; Heb. 1:2).

John wrote again with pristine clarity of the deity of the Word, our Lord. In John 1:4 he said, "In Him was life." This is an amazing statement. The One whom we know as Jesus was and is, in John's words, the author and source of all life. Since the giving of life to all things in the creation narrative

---

I–XII, Anchor Bible (New York: Doubleday, 1966), 4; Leon Morris, *The Gospel according to John*, New International Commentary on the New Testament (1971; repr., Grand Rapids: Eerdmans, 1989), 72–73; Herman Ridderbos, *The Gospel of John: A Theological Commentary*, trans. John Vriend (Grand Rapids: Eerdmans, 1997), 24–25.

of Genesis 1 is the prerogative of God alone, there could be no clearer way for John to say that our Lord Jesus is divine than by saying He is also the source of all spiritual life in this age of new creation.

Songs of the Savior
The ancient people of God also sang about the deity of our Lord in the Psalms. For instance, Psalm 2 exalts the Lord and His anointed—the King and His Son (vv. 6–7). This Son, begotten of the Father, is given the nations as an inheritance (vv. 7–8) as well as the right to judge the ungodly (v. 9). The Epistle to the Hebrews picks up on this and quotes Psalm 2:7,

> You are My Son,
> Today I have begotten you,

in the context of exalting Jesus over the angels. Before quoting the psalmist's words, the inspired writer points out that God never said to any angel what He said to Jesus. Elsewhere, the apostle Paul applies the statement that the Son was begotten of the Father in Psalm 2 to the resurrection of Jesus from the dead (Acts 13:33). Yet the author of Hebrews applies it to the point that Jesus is divine while the angels are not.

Elsewhere in the Psalms, the sons of Korah sing of the loveliness of the king, calling him to gird His sword and ride out in victory as the Mighty One (45:3–4). Then they exalt the king, saying,

> Your throne, O God, is forever and ever….
> Therefore God, Your God, has anointed You. (vv. 6, 7)

What they said of the earthly king of Israel in grandiose terms is true of our Lord Jesus, the true king of the people of

God from heaven. According to Hebrews 1:8–9 these words were spoken by God the Father of His Son.

Finally, Psalm 110:1 opens with the declaration,

> The LORD said to my Lord,
> "Sit at My right hand,
> Till I make Your enemies Your footstool."

Like the author of Hebrews, we ask, "To which of the angels" did God ever say this? Prophetically our Lord was praised by the Lord's people in this psalm as the one at the place of authority and power at the right hand of God.

Isaiah Saw His Glory

Later in redemptive history, we are given an even clearer glimpse of who Jesus is. One proof of His deity is found in the famous words of Isaiah 6:1–3:

> I saw the Lord sitting on a throne, high and lifted up, and the train of His robe filled the temple. Above it stood seraphim; each one had six wings: with two he covered his face, with two he covered his feet, and with two he flew. And one cried to another and said:
>
> > "Holy, holy, holy is the LORD of hosts;
> > The whole earth is full of His glory!"

How is this passage a proof of Jesus's divinity? John interprets the prophet's words in chapter 12 of his gospel account. After chronicling the signs that Christ did and the continuing unbelief of the people, the apostle quotes from Isaiah 53:1 and 6:10 to show that the prophet foretold their unbelief. After quoting Isaiah 6:10, John comments, "These things Isaiah said when he saw His glory and spoke of Him" (John 12:41).

The "His" John refers to is Jesus Christ. What a connection! Isaiah "saw" the Lord (or, a visible accommodation to Isaiah's capacity), who was high and lifted up in transcendent glory, whose robe filled the temple in immanent presence, and whom the seraphim *worshiped* (Isa. 6:1–3). All these things speak of divinity. John says this was God the Son before His incarnation as the Lord Jesus Christ. Isaiah saw the glory of the One who would be called, "Wonderful, Counselor, Mighty God" (Isa. 9:6). This image of the glory of the Lord in Isaiah's vision is why Paul called Jesus "the Lord of glory" (1 Cor. 2:8) and why John sees the Lord with white hair, eyes like flames, and feet like refined bronze (Rev. 1:12–16 ESV).

Prepare the Way of the Lord
In Isaiah 40, we read that the Lord Himself would come to save His people. These words spoke comfort to the languishing people of God. At the end of her warfare (v. 2), Jerusalem would see the greatest possible sign: "Behold your God!" (v. 9). Because of this promise, Isaiah called the people to prepare a way for the Lord in the desert (v. 3), for the glory of the Lord would be revealed and all flesh would see it (v. 5). The New Testament interprets these words for us (Matt. 3:1–12; Mark 1:1–11; Luke 3:1–22). The "voice" that Isaiah said would cry out in the wilderness was John the Baptist (or Baptizer). The Lord to come was none other than our Lord Jesus Christ, Judah's God, the glory of the Lord incarnated: "And we beheld His glory, the glory as of the only begotten of the Father, full of grace and truth" (John 1:14). What's interesting is that in Isaiah 40:3 the voice cries out,

> Make straight in the desert
> A highway for our God.

In Mark 1, the gospel writer quotes this passage from Isaiah and, with Spirit-anointed authority, reveals that John the Baptist is crying out, "Make *His* paths straight." Who is the "His" of verse 3? Mark continues, "It came to pass in those days that Jesus came" (v. 9).

> On Jordan's bank the Baptist's cry
> announces that the Lord is nigh.
> Awake and harken, for he brings
> glad tidings of the King of kings!
>
> Then cleansed be every life from sin:
> make straight the way for God within,
> and let us all our hearts prepare
> for Christ to come and enter there.[7]

His Goings Forth Are from of Old

We also have the prophetic testimony of Isaiah's contemporary Micah in mid-seventh century BC. In a time when God's people had degenerate kings and the day was coming when the kingly line of David would be cut down like a tree stump, Micah spoke of the kingship's return. This king, though, would be no ordinary king. He wouldn't be a king from the merely mortal line of David, coming with great expectation but eventually dying in disappointment. Micah referred to Israel's coming king when he prophesied of

---

7. Charles Coffin, "On Jordan's Bank the Baptist's Cry," in *Worship and Rejoice* (Carol Stream, Ill.: Hope Publishing, 2001), #156.

the One to be Ruler in Israel
Whose goings forth are from of old,
From everlasting. (5:2)[8]

This king would not just rule like God with divine authority but would Himself be eternal God and therefore the people's true Savior. When the magi came from the East to offer the newborn king gifts, they perceived His true nature: "Where is He who has been born King of the Jews? For we have seen His star in the East and have come to worship Him" (Matt. 2:2).

His Deity in the New Testament

Thus it happened that this glorious king was born in order to save His people. Pause for a moment and reflect on how difficult it must have been for those first Jews who heard this message to believe it. Put yourself in their shoes. People like Timothy had been taught the Old Testament Scriptures "from childhood" (2 Tim. 3:15). He learned that it was blasphemy (cursing God) to claim that anyone or anything other than Yahweh, the Lord of the covenant between Israel and Him, was the Savior. He learned the first of the Ten Commandments: "You shall have no other gods before Me" (Ex. 20:3). He learned how the prophets of Israel interpreted these words:

---

8. Some modern translations render this "from ancient days" (ESV) and "from ancient times" (CSB and NIV), referring to the Davidic kingdom. On this meaning, see Leslie C. Allen, *The Books of Joel, Obadiah, Jonah and Micah*, New International Commentary on the Old Testament (Grand Rapids: Eerdmans, 1976), 342–44. On the older understanding that this refers to the eternal deity of this king, see C. F. Keil, *The Minor Prophets*, vol. 10 of *Commentary on the Old Testament* (1866–1891; repr., Peabody, Mass.: Hendrickson, 1996), 324–26.

I, even I, am the LORD,
And besides Me there is no savior. (Isa. 43:11)

Yet I am the LORD your God
Ever since the land of Egypt,
And you shall know no God but Me;
For there is no savior besides Me. (Hos. 13:4)

He Will Save His People from Their Sins

Yet we cross that chasm between Old and New Testaments in our Bibles and hear that the Holy One within Mary's womb was to be named "JESUS, for He will save His people from their sins" (Matt. 1:21). "Jesus" is our Anglicized transliteration of the Greek *Iēsous* (Ἰησοῦς), which was based on the Hebrew *yeshua* (יֵשׁוּעַ), "Yahweh [the Lord] saves." Jesus's name signified who He was. Thus, the apostles could say to a Jewish audience, "Nor is there salvation in any other, for there is no other name under heaven given among men by which we must be saved" (Acts 4:12). Jesus is the Lord who the prophets said was coming to save! Because of this, Paul said that, as the incarnate Son, Jesus is the "one Mediator between God and men" (1 Tim. 2:5). The apostles confidently preached and wrote about Jesus Christ being the Savior (2 Tim. 1:10; Titus 1:4; 2:13; 3:6; 2 Peter 1:11; 2:20; 3:18).

Before Abraham Was Born, "I Am"

After the Savior-King was born, He was wrapped in the "royal garb" of swaddling cloths and "enthroned" in an animal trough (Luke 2:7). Later, during His earthly ministry, our Lord debated with the Pharisees, the wise men of His day. In one of His great debates, He unequivocally proclaimed

Himself God. The Pharisees had just accused Him of being demon possessed and asked Him the question, "Are You greater than our father Abraham, who is dead?" (John 8:53). Jesus responded without hesitation: "Abraham rejoiced to see My day, and he saw it and was glad" (v. 56). How could this be? Jesus was only about thirty years old, and Abraham had died thousands of years before. Jesus answered that too: "Most assuredly [literally, "Amen, amen"], I say to you, before Abraham was, I AM" (v. 58).

If you know the story of the Old Testament, you'll recognize that phrase "I AM." The Lord proclaimed that He was the great "I AM" who revealed Himself to Moses at the burning bush (Ex. 3:14). At that burning bush, the I AM said He was the God of Abraham, Isaac, and Jacob (vv. 6, 15). So when the Pharisees said they were the children of Abraham, Jesus calls Himself "I AM" (*egō eimi*), the God of Abraham! To do this, He remarkably uses the same phrase the ancient Greek translation of the Hebrew Old Testament (called the Septuagint) uses for the great "I AM" of Exodus 3. Not only did this show that our Lord was "mighty in the Scriptures" (Acts 18:24; cf. Luke 2:46–47), evidencing His intricate knowledge, but also that He spoke as one with authority (Matt. 7:29; Mark 1:22) to interpret the Scriptures as finding their fulfillment in Him (John 5:37; Luke 4:21; 24:27, 44–47).

My Lord and My God!
After His glorious resurrection "according to the Scriptures" (1 Cor. 15:4; cf. Nicene Creed), the glorified Lord and King appeared to His downcast disciples, especially "doubting" Thomas. When the other disciples told Thomas that they had

seen the Lord Jesus alive from the dead, he responded that unless he could see with his own eyes and touch with his own hands the wounds of Jesus, he would not believe (John 20:25). (God is always up for challenges like these! If you're reading this and you're a skeptic or seeker, ask God to reveal Himself to you as you consider His word.) Thus, it came to pass eight days later that Jesus again appeared to His disciples. This time Thomas was among them. Standing in their midst, Jesus looked directly into Thomas's eyes and commanded him to touch His crucifixion wounds and believe. To this, Thomas cried out in amazing clarity, "My Lord and my God!" (John 20:28).

Resembling the Son of God
The writer of the Epistle to the Hebrews also testifies of the Son's eternality in an intriguing statement. In Hebrews 7:3, the author says that the enigmatic and shadowy Old Testament priest-king Melchizedek (cf. Gen. 14:17–24) was "made like" or "resembling" (ESV) the Son of God. How? Melchizedek didn't have a familial genealogy or account of his birth or death recorded in Scripture. Similarly, the Son truly has "neither beginning of days nor end of life." Note well here that Hebrews isn't saying that the Son, Jesus Christ, resembled Melchizedek. This would mean Melchizedek was an Old Testament type pointing *forward* in the annals of time to the birth of the Son of God. Instead, Hebrews says that Melchizedek "resembled" the Son. This means that the Son was the eternal and original archetype whose person and work intruded on human history at various times. Melchizedek, then, was not a foreshadowing of Jesus, but rather the Son cast down *His shadow* from heaven to earth in the person of Melchizedek. Melchizedek

was an earthly and temporal figure of the heavenly and eternal Son of God.[9] Jesus is that Son!

He Upholds the Universe
Not only is the Son of God the one through whom all things were made but He is also the one who providentially cares for all that He has made. We usually associate the work of God's providence with the Father. For example, in question 27, the Heidelberg Catechism says,

> What dost thou understand by the Providence of God?
>
> The almighty and every where present power of God, whereby, as it were by his hand, he still upholds heaven and earth, with all creatures, and so governs them that herbs and grass, rain and drought, fruitful and barren years, meat and drink, health and sickness, riches and poverty, yea, all things, come not by chance, but by his fatherly hand.[10]

Also, the New Testament teaches that the Son participates in the divine work of providence since He's coequal and coeternal with God the Father and the Spirit. After stating that through the Son of God all things were created and that He's the radiance of God's glory and the exact imprint of His nature, the inspired writer says that He is "upholding [present tense] all things by the word of His power" (Heb. 1:3). "In the beginning" (Gen. 1:1) God the Father spoke His omnipotent decree and all things came into being through the Son.

---

9. Geerhardus Vos, *The Teaching of the Epistle to the Hebrews*, ed. Johannes G. Vos (1956; repr., Eugene, Ore.: Wipf & Stock, 1998), 49–87.

10. Schaff, *Creeds*, 2:316.

Hebrews tells us that our Lord continues to speak a powerful word of providence.

This text is illuminated by a story from the Gospel of John. When Jesus said "rise" and healed a man who had an infirmity thirty-eight years, then told him "take up your bed and walk" (5:8), the Judean leaders sought to kill him (v. 16). Why? Because he healed on the Sabbath (v. 9). While the Lord's command forbade work (Ex. 20:8–11), the tradition of the elders of Israel interpreted this to include carrying something from one place to another. What's telling is how the leadership charged Jesus with breaking the command and not the man who took up his mat and walked away with it. Jesus told His accusers, "My Father has been working until now, and I have been working" (John 5:17). He's speaking of the work of upholding the universe in His providence.[11]

Hebrews 1:3 is also explained by Paul's hymn to Christ (Col. 1:15–20). The "Son of [the Father's] love" (v. 13) is said to be the one "by [whom] all things were created that are in heaven and that are on earth, visible and invisible…. All things were created through Him and for Him" (v. 16). The Son is the Creator. Then Paul says He is the Sustainer: "in Him all things consist" (v. 17). The form of the verb "consist" (*sunestēken*) is a perfect active indicative: "in Him all things *are being held together*" constantly. In other words, there's not one stray atom, molecule, quark, or particle unknown to Him in the universe because our Lord is sustaining them all in His providential power.

---

11. See the discussion in Carson, *Gospel according to John*, 244–45.

The Son of God: Christ's Divine Nature

He Is the True God

In 1 John 5:20 we find one of the clearest statements that Jesus the Son is fully divine. John states that the purpose of his book is that his readers might have the assurance of fellowship with the Father and His Son (1 John 1:1–4). At the end of the epistle John says,

> And we know that the Son of God has come and has given us an understanding, that we may know Him who is true; and we are in Him who is true, in His Son Jesus Christ. This is the true God and eternal life. (1 John 5:20)

John tells us that if we're in the Son then we're in the Father. To be "in" means to have fellowship with Father and Son. The reason we know that having fellowship with the Son means having fellowship with the Father is because His Son Jesus "is the true God and eternal life." Amazing! The next verse, which is the last verse of 1 John, is also striking: "Little children, keep yourselves from idols" (5:21). If Jesus weren't God, He would be an idol! Yet John has just said that Jesus is "*the true God*" and life everlasting!

The Alpha and the Omega

The final book of the Bible—Revelation—offers a clear affirmation of the deity of Jesus Christ. After "the Lord…the Almighty" declares Himself to be "Alpha" and "Omega," "Beginning" and "End" (1:8), John then turns to "see" the voice he heard (v. 12). When he did, he "fell at His feet as dead" (v. 17). He was in the presence of One who is awesome and majestic. This glorious One then lays His right hand on John and comforts him, saying, "*I* am the First and the Last. *I* am He who lives, and was dead, and, behold, I am alive forevermore. Amen" (vv. 17–18). If "the Lord…the Almighty" in verse 8 is the Father, then in verses 17–18 Jesus is equating Himself with the Father by using these descriptions. If verse 8 and verses 17–18 are both Jesus speaking, then He's calling Himself God as well. Regardless of which way we understand this, John records that Jesus is God! Finally, at the end of Revelation Jesus says, "I am the Alpha and the Omega, the Beginning and the End…. I am the Alpha and the Omega, the Beginning and the End, the First and the Last" (21:6; 22:13).

In these designations, the Father and Jesus are speaking the words of the Lord Himself from the prophet Isaiah's writings. When the prophet comforted exiled and deserted Israel, the Lord told Israel not to fear, for He is the one who raised up their oppressor:

> I, the LORD, am the first;
> And with the last I am He. (Isa. 41:4)

Later He calls Israel to be His witnesses:

> Before Me there was no God formed,
> Nor shall there be after Me.
> I, even I, am the LORD,
> And besides Me there is no savior. (Isa. 43:10–11)

Finally, Jesus's words in Revelation are the Lord's words:

> Thus says the LORD, the King of Israel,
> And his Redeemer, the LORD of hosts:
> "I am the First and I am the Last;
> Besides Me there is no God." (Isa. 44:6)

Theological Reasons for Jesus's Divinity
The Attributes of God
The Bible's testimony of Jesus Christ being the divine Lord is extensive. Added to the impressive list of texts from Genesis through Revelation already mentioned are the general theological truths showing that Jesus shares the same attributes as God the Father. He's omnipresent (Matt. 28:20; Eph. 1:23; 4:10), immutable (Mal. 3:6; Heb. 13:8), omniscient even to the point of hearing our prayers and knowing our thoughts (Acts 1:24; 7:59; Rom. 10:13), and omnipotent (Matt. 28:18; 1 Cor. 15:27; Eph. 1:22; Rev. 1:4; 19:16). He's also spoken of as the final judge of the living and the dead on the last day of human history (2 Cor. 5:10). In short, whatever it means to be God, Jesus is.

The Only Begotten Son
The New Testament also emphasizes the deity of Christ by using the title *monogenēs*, which renders John 3:16 mostly in older translations as "only begotten Son" (KJV, NASB95, NKJV) and in more modern versions as "one and only Son" (CSB, NIV) and "only Son" (ESV, RSV). For the eternal Father to have a Son means the Son is as eternal as the Father.

In the opening of John's gospel, we read of the incarnate Word's "glory" (*doxa*; 1:14), which in the Old Testament is a term that is equated with the majesty of God:

> They shall see the glory of the LORD,
> The excellency of our God. (Isa. 35:2;
>   cf. 1 Chron. 29:11; Job 40:10)

John says this glory of the incarnate Word was "of the only begotten of the Father" (1:14). This glory of the only begotten is because the Word, our Lord Jesus, is "the only begotten Son, who is in the bosom of the Father" (v. 18). Since "the only begotten Son" shares intimate fellowship in glory with the Father in eternity, John makes that even more remarkable claim that He has "declared," or made known, this unseen God (v. 18). This is what Jesus Himself would go on to say during His earthly ministry: "All things have been delivered to Me by My Father, and no one knows the Son except the Father. Nor does anyone know the Father except the Son, and the one to whom the Son wills to reveal Him" (Matt. 11:27; cf. Heb. 1:2).

The Same Substance with the Father

What does it mean that Jesus is the only begotten Son? The consensus of the historic Christian church is that "only begotten" means that Jesus Christ, the Son of God, is fully God. For example, Theognostus (ca. 260), a leader in the church in Alexandria, said,

> The substance of the Son is not a substance devised extraneously, nor is it one introduced out of nothing; but it was born of the substance of the Father, as the reflection of light or as the steam of water. For the reflection is not the sun itself, and the steam is not the water itself, nor yet again is it anything alien; neither He Himself the Father, nor is He alien, but He is an emanation from the substance of the Father, this substance of the Father suffering the while no partition. For as the sun remains the same and suffers no diminution from the rays that are poured out by it, so neither did the

substance of the Father undergo any change in having the Son as an image of itself.[12]

During those early centuries in the Christian church, a great struggle for the biblical doctrine of the deity of the Son ensued. There were those in the ancient church who redefined what it meant to say that the Son was the Son of the Father. The Ebionites, the Alogi, and Dynamic Monarchians all rejected the deity of Christ. Because of these heresies, the great Council of Nicea (Nicea is now the city of Iznik in modern-day Turkey) convened in 325. This first ecumenical (universal/worldwide) council of the Christian church met from May 20 to July 25 in order to respond to the teaching of Arius (ca. 250–336), a popular preacher. He popularized his theology into music as well as into simplistic syllogistic reasoning, which said that since all sons have a beginning, therefore the Son also had to have a beginning:

The Father is older than the Son,
The Father is greater than the Son,
Therefore, the Son is less than the Father.

Arius taught that the Son was of a different (*hetero*) substance (*ousia*) from the Father. Another church father at the same council, Eusebius (263–339), tried to mediate and soften this teaching with a compromise: the Son was of a like (*homoi*) substance (*ousia*) with the Father. On the opposite side of Arius was Athanasius (293–373), a deacon in the church in

---

12. Theognostus, *Seven Books of Hypotyposes or Outlines I*, in *Ante-Nicene Fathers*, ed. Alexander Roberts and James Donaldson, rev. A. Cleveland Coxe, trans. S. D. Salmond (1885; repr., Peabody, Mass.: Hendrickson, 2004), 6:155.

Alexandria. As the story goes, when Athanasius learned that the world was against him and that he stood alone in supporting the doctrine of the Son's "same substance" with the Father, he gave his famous reply, "If the world is against Athanasius, then Athanasius is against the world" (*contra mundum*). He taught that the Son was of the same (*homo*) substance (*ousia*) with the Father. Jesus Himself refers to this truth in John 10:27–30, speaking of Himself as the Shepherd who gives life to His sheep. This alone testifies to His deity, as no one gives life except God. Jesus continues: "Neither shall anyone snatch them out of My hand.... No one is able to snatch them out of My Father's hand. I and My Father are one" (vv. 28–30). Their oneness is not just in will and purpose but in essence. If the Son gives life just like the Father and if the Son preserves His sheep just like the Father, then they're equally the author and preserver of eternal life. They're both God. Throughout the New Testament this truth is affirmed:

> I could wish that I myself were accursed from Christ for my brethren...of whom [the Israelites] are the fathers and from whom, according to the flesh, Christ came, who is over all, the eternally blessed God. Amen. (Rom. 9:3, 5)

But to the Son He says:

> "Your throne, O God, is forever and ever;
> A scepter of righteousness is the scepter of Your kingdom.
> You have loved righteousness and hated lawlessness;
> Therefore God, Your God, has anointed You
> With the oil of gladness more than Your companions."
> (Heb. 1:8–9)

> Simon Peter, a bondservant and apostle of Jesus Christ,
>
> To those who have obtained like precious faith with us by the righteousness of our God and Savior Jesus Christ. (2 Peter 1:1)
>
> For in [Christ] dwells all the fullness of the Godhead bodily. (Col. 2:9)

Because of this unequivocal teaching, Christ's deity is confessed in all the great creeds of the historic, orthodox Christian church. No religious group, therefore, can validly call themselves Christian unless they proclaim the deity of Christ. The resulting document of the council that met in Nicea in 325 is called the Nicene Creed. Whereas the Apostles' Creed uses the simple language of Scripture when confessing of Christ, "I believe in Jesus Christ, His only begotten Son," the Council of Nicea was forced to elaborate on this biblical affirmation because of doctrinal controversy. Jesus is "begotten of the Father before all worlds [God of God], Light of Light, very God of very God, begotten, not made, being of one substance [essence] with the Father; by whom all things were made."[13]

Eternally Begotten

"Before all worlds" or "ages" is the language used in the Nicene Creed. The statement that Jesus is begotten of the Father "before all worlds" is the heart of the affirmation of the Son's eternality. Recalling what was said in the introduction to this book, we must recognize that the language God inspired in Scripture and that we use in our theological

---

13. Schaff, *Creeds*, 2:58–59.

speech is an accommodation to us ignorant sinners. As an example, the words "Father" and "Son" beautifully evoke the intimate relationship of love that exists between a father and his firstborn son. Because of this language, church history is filled with those such as Arians and Jehovah's Witnesses who reason that because the Bible speaks of the Son, He therefore had to have been begotten by the Father at some time. This is logical, isn't it? After all, when we look at the world around us we see men become husbands and husbands become fathers in due course. Notice how the Athanasian Creed answers this unbiblical logic: "The Son is of the Father alone: not made nor created: but begotten.... God, of the Substance [Essence] of the Father; begotten before the worlds (§§22, 31).[14] Has the Son always existed? Yes. Was He created? No. The Belgic Confession of Faith simply follows the creeds, saying, "We believe that Jesus Christ, according to his divine nature, is the only begotten Son of God, begotten from eternity.... [He] is the Son of God, not only from the time that he assumed our nature, but from all eternity" (art. 10).[15] Because the Son of God is eternally begotten, the Belgic Confession makes this conclusion: He was "not made nor created (for then he would be a creature), but co-essential and co-eternal with the Father, the express image of his person and the brightness of his glory, equal unto him in all things" (art. 10).[16]

This is the doctrine of the eternal generation of the Son. What does it mean that the Son is "eternally begotten"? Our

---

14. See Appendix 1: The Ecumenical Creeds.

15. Schaff, *Creeds*, 3:393. On Belgic Confession, art. 10, see Hyde, *With Heart and Mouth*, 137–42.

16. Schaff, *Creeds*, 3:393.

minds cannot fully comprehend it, but we apprehend it by faith like little children. The language of "begetting" is that of a child being born to a father, but the Son is "eternally" begotten. The Son has always been the Son, the Father has always been the Father, and they have always loved, communed, and fellowshipped with one another. As the Belgic Confession says, "Therefore it must needs follow that he—who is called God, the Word, the Son, and Jesus Christ—did exist at that time when all things were created by him" (art. 10).[17]

This is an affirmation of the Athanasian Creed, which says that Christ's divine nature is "God, of the substance [essence] of the Father; begotten before the worlds...perfect God...equal to the Father as touching his Godhead" (§§31, 32, 33).[18] Thus our Lord Jesus Christ is as truly and fully God as God the Father, being eternally begotten by Him and one substance with Him.

In confessing this, we believe the ancient Christian faith against Adoptionism. This is a belief that Christ, a divine being, adopted a man named Jesus. The church rejected this belief very early, yet it emerged again in the seventh and eighth centuries in Spain, which was on the outskirts of the Roman/Christian Empire. In 675, the Council of Toledo declared, "This Son of God is also Son by nature, not by adoption."[19] As Reformed Christians, we follow this ancient declaration in the Heidelberg Catechism, which explains,

---

17. Schaff, *Creeds*, 3:394.
18. See Appendix 1: The Ecumenical Creeds.
19. Jacques Dupuis and Josef Neuner, eds., *The Christian Faith: In the Doctrinal Documents of the Catholic Church* (New York: Alba House, 1982), 103.

Why is he called God's only begotten Son, since we also are the children of God?

Because Christ alone is the eternal natural Son of God; but we are children of God by adoption through grace for his sake.[20]

Conclusion

All this is to say that the Old and the New Testaments proclaim the true and full divinity of Jesus the Messiah, the Son of God, who acted in creation and redemption. Furthermore, the ancient church expressed this doctrine in its creeds that arose from its many-sided doctrinal disputes. The importance of this doctrine can't be overstated. In the words of John Owen, "Take this away, and all our religion is taken away with it. Farewell Christianity, as to the mystery, the glory, the truth, the efficacy of it;—let a refined heathenism be established in its room."[21]

> Christ, by highest heaven adored,
> Christ, the Everlasting Lord!
> Late in time behold Him come,
> Offspring of the Virgin's womb.
> Veiled in flesh the Godhead see;
> Hail th'Incarnate Deity,
> Pleased as man with men to dwell,
> Jesus, our Emmanuel.
> Hark! the herald angels sing,
> "Glory to the newborn King."[22]

---

20. Dupuis and Neuner, *Christian Faith*, 3:318.
21. Owen, *Meditations and Discourses on the Glory of Christ*, in *Works*, 1:328.
22. Charles Wesley, "Hark! the Herald Angels Sing," in *Psalter Hymnal*, #339.

FOUR

The Son of Man: Christ's Human Nature

> For there is one God and one Mediator between God and men, the Man Christ Jesus.
> —1 TIMOTHY 2:5

"What if God was one of us?" Singer Joan Osborne posed one of the most interesting questions of the ages in her 1996 one-hit wonder. Yet this song portrayed a certain angst and conundrum when the singer asked what God's face would look like if He had one. And would you want to see God's face if it meant

> that you would have to believe in things like heaven
> And in Jesus and the saints, and all the prophets?

If we really want to meet God face-to-face, we and our beliefs will never be the same. God *has* become one of us, so much so that He did have a face with ordinary definable features like you and I have. Knowing this changes everything and inevitably leads to believing certain things—about Jesus, the saints, and all the prophets.

While the deity of the Lord Jesus Christ has been one of the strong emphases of evangelical Christianity for generations, one unintended result has been neglecting the truth of

His humanity. One reason for the emphasis on the deity of Christ was that in the early twentieth century the modernists, also called liberals, stressed that Jesus was a mere man. According to Friedrich Schleiermacher (1768–1834), Jesus was a man with a supreme God-consciousness; for Albrecht Ritschl (1822–1889), He was a man with the value of a god; for Albert Schweitzer (1875–1965), He was an eschatological prophet. Against these ideas, the fundamentalists of the early twentieth century reasserted Jesus's deity.

Even non-Christians have believed that Jesus existed and that He was man, so Jesus's humanity seems obvious to us. But Jesus's humanity is a necessary topic to consider since He has two natures. It's the human nature of Jesus that I'll address in this chapter because it leads us to the answer to the question, What if God was one of us?

The Reality of the Incarnation

Is it just pious rhetoric to say that God really became one with us in our humanity? After all, weren't the Greek philosophers correct in saying that it was a bad thing to be made of flesh and that the body is the prison of the soul? Just how real was this supposed incarnation? How human was (or is) Jesus Christ? The Belgic Confession explains the reality of the human nature of Christ, saying that the Son became man by "really assuming the true human nature, with all its infirmities, sin excepted, being conceived in the womb of the blessed Virgin Mary, by the power of the Holy Ghost, without the means of man; and did not only assume human nature as to the body, but also a true human soul, that he might be a real man" (art. 18).[1]

Jesus has a true human nature, meaning He possesses the peculiar qualities, attributes, and characteristics of being human. What are these? In general, He has a human body and a human soul so "that He might be a real man." He assumed everything that makes us human. The only difference between Christ's humanity and ours is that He was and is "without sin" (Heb. 4:15).[2] The reality of the incarnation is what the simple affirmation "the Word became flesh" (John 1:14) communicates. Also, Hebrews 2:14, 17 says, "Inasmuch then as the children have partaken of flesh and blood, He himself likewise shared in the same, that through death He might destroy him who had the power of death, that is, the devil.... Therefore, in all things He had to be made like His brethren, that He might be a merciful and faithful High Priest in things pertaining to God, to make propitiation for the sins of the people."

When discussing the incarnation, it's important to grasp that the Son of God didn't assume an existing human *being*, as if He came from heaven and possessed a lifeless corpse. This is what the opening illustrations of this book tend toward in their zeal to communicate this mystery in ordinary ways: He put on humanity like a coat, or He was "all God *in a bod*." Instead, ancient theologians such as John of Damascus (b. 676) pointed out that the eternal Logos, the Son of God, assumed a *potential human*—that is, a human nature that hadn't yet developed. This means that from conception until birth, the

---

1. Schaff, *Creeds*, 3:402–3.
2. Athanasius, *On the Incarnation*, 4:40.

human nature of Christ had to grow and develop through all the stages of gestation just like ours.³ As the account of Luke 2 states, after His circumcision "the Child grew and became strong in spirit, filled with wisdom" (v. 40) and "increased in wisdom and stature, and in favor with God and men" (v. 52). When Mary conceived, the child within her had to go through all the stages of life. To say it as reverently but realistically as possible, the Son of God became a blastocyst, a zygote, a fetus, an infant, a toddler, a child, and an adolescent before entering His public ministry as an adult. As we'll see in chapter 5, this means we can say that the Creator was nursed, the providential Lord who cared for all creation had His diaper changed, the eternal Son who perfectly existed with the Father and the Spirit had to make friends, the immense Son had to grow, the infinitely wise Son had to learn, and the omnipotent Son had to increase in strength. To speak more properly, the incarnated Creator, the Son-in-flesh experienced these things. But I'll deal with that point in the next chapter.

Our Lord came so far to save us that He was willing to become everything that we've been, are now, and will be in the future. This means the person of the Son added a human nature, *not* a human person. The ancient fathers spoke of the "impersonal" (*anhypostasia*) or "inpersonal" (*enhypostasia*)

---

3. This is contrary to the esteemed Reformation Old Testament scholar Johannes Wollebius, who seemingly wanted to honor the sanctity of the humanity of our Lord to the extent that he said the body of our Lord "was completed at once, and not over a period of time like the bodies of other men.... Whereas in ordinary generation the time required for formation of the body is forty days, the body of Christ was absolutely completed in a moment. Otherwise Christ would have been conceived not as a man but as an embryo." *Compendium Theologiae Christianae*, 89–90.

character of Christ's human nature. The human nature did not have a separate existence apart from the incarnation that the Son entered into. Instead, from the moment of conception, the human nature of Christ existed in the person of the Son of God.

The Basic Affirmations

We see the reality of the incarnation assumed throughout the New Testament. The picture given to us by the evangelists is that our Lord was a true man. He called Himself a man (John 8:40), as did others (Acts 2:22; Rom. 5:15; 1 Cor. 15:21). He had a human genealogy that records the names of His human ancestors (Matthew 1; Luke 3). He was of the seed of Abraham, meaning He was Jewish (Gal. 3:16). His family line was that of the tribe of Judah and the house of David (Rom. 1:3; Heb. 7:14; Rev. 5:5; 22:16). He was born of a woman (Gal. 4:4) in a Jewish city, Bethlehem (Luke 2:4, 6), as the oldest child of Mary and her husband, Joseph, the carpenter. He was circumcised (Luke 2:21; Rom. 15:8). He grew up in a historical town, Nazareth (Acts 2:22; 3:6). He had brothers (1 Cor. 9:5; Gal. 1:19). We've also seen that He had to grow in wisdom and in stature just like all other boys, being subject to the ordinary laws of human development (Luke 2:40, 52). Further, the Epistle to the Hebrews expresses the true humanity of our Lord in this way: "He learned obedience by the things which He suffered" (5:8; cf. 2:10, 18). Christ's human nature was true. This means it was created, had a beginning of days, was finite, and retained all the properties of a true human nature.

A Real Body

We confess Christ's true humanity, but we may question how real His body was. Did He really have human flesh and blood as we do? Did He need to sleep like us? We confess that He really assumed, or took on Himself, a human body. As said above, Jesus's body grew from an embryo, to a fetus, to a baby, to a toddler, all the way to a full-grown man. The necessity of the Son of God taking on Himself a true human body from conception to maturation was that He might truly become one of us as "God *with* us." Since we move throughout all the stages of life, so too our Lord was "made like His brethren" (Heb. 2:17), growing and maturing as our Mediator. In the words of the Belgic Confession, His body has "not lost its properties, but remained a creature, having beginning of days, being a finite nature, and retaining all the properties of a real body. And though he hath by his resurrection given immortality to the same, nevertheless he hath not changed the reality of his human nature; forasmuch as our salvation and resurrection also depend on the reality of his body" (art. 19).[4]

Scripture abounds with affirmations of the true humanity of Christ, including the true body of Christ. For example, Jesus experienced hunger after fasting forty days and nights (e.g., Matt. 4:2). He experienced exhaustion after a day of traveling, teaching, and healing (Matt. 8:24; Mark 4:38; John 4:6). He experienced agony in the garden of Gethsemane (Luke 22:44). He experienced thirst, especially on the cross (John 4:7; 19:28). He experienced true human pain (e.g., 1 Peter 2:21–23). He experienced death (e.g., Phil. 2:8).

---

4. Schaff, *Creeds*, 3:404.

The Bible uses language in a way that may confuse us, however, when it says the Son came "in the *likeness* of sinful flesh" (Rom. 8:3; cf. Phil. 2:7). We must ask what "likeness" means. Does it mean that Jesus had a human nature like us, but that it was not exactly like us? Paul's use of "likeness" (*homoiōma*) in these texts denotes that there was no real sinfulness in the human nature of Christ, yet He came not only as a man in our human flesh but like men who are sinners. As the great Princeton theologian Charles Hodge (1797–1878) said, "Christ took our physically dilapidated nature, subject to the infirmities which sin had brought into it. He was therefore susceptible of pain, and weariness, and sorrow."[5] Paul describes the human body as being a "lowly body" (*to sōma tēs tapeinōseōs*; Phil. 3:21). "Lowly" here is also translated as "the body of our humiliation" (ASV), "the body of our lowly condition" (NASB), or simply "lowly bodies" (NIV). Thus, the Son came into a completely weak situation, yet He was without sin. He came to earth in a human body "just like" ours, not into "something like" our human flesh.[6]

The beloved disciple of Jesus says in 1 John 1:1 that he and the followers of Jesus with "our hands have handled... the Word of life"—the same eternal, life-giving Logos he wrote of in John 1:1–4. As well, John condemns as the spirit

---

5. Charles Hodge, *A Commentary on Romans*, Geneva Series of Commentaries (1835; repr., Edinburgh: Banner of Truth, 1989), 252–53.

6. The question of whether Christ got sick is not answered by Scripture. So when Isaiah 53:4 says, "surely He has borne our griefs and carried our sorrows," Matthew 8:17 says this was fulfilled in Christ's healing ministry: "He Himself took our infirmities and bore our sicknesses." He had a post-fall body just like ours. So the possibility/probability of Christ suffering sickness should not be ruled out, yet though He had a post-fall body, He was sinless.

of antichrist anyone who denies that the incarnation has taken place (1 John 2:18, 23; 4:3; 2 John 7).

A Real Soul

We recognize that Jesus really assumed a true human body. But did He assume a true human soul? We confess this as true also, saying that He also assumed "a true human soul, that He might be a real man" (Belgic Confession, art. 18). He had to possess the immaterial part of us in order to be truly human. In the story of the creation of Adam, God formed a body from the dust, and after He "breathed into his nostrils the breath of life," this man "became a living soul" (Gen. 2:7 KJV). These two elements—body and soul—made Adam a human being. In order to be the second Adam, Jesus had to be truly human; He had to have both a body and a soul. Thus our Lord spoke of this immaterial aspect of His humanity when He said, "My soul [*psuchē*] is exceedingly sorrowful, even to death" (Matt. 26:38) and, "Father, 'into Your hands I commit My spirit'" (*pneuma*; Luke 23:46; cf. Matt. 27:50; John 19:30).[7]

Traditionally, historic, orthodox Christians have described the true humanity of Jesus Christ, saying that He is a man "made of the substance [essence] of his mother, born in the world...perfect man, of a reasonable soul and human flesh subsisting...inferior to the Father as touching his manhood" (Athanasian Creed, §§31, 32, 33).[8] Confessing that Christ has

---

7. The biblical terms "soul" and "spirit" are synonymous. For a brief explanation and defense of this position, see John Murray, "Trichotomy," in *Systematic Theology*, vol. 2 of *Collected Writings of John Murray* (1977; repr., Edinburgh: Banner of Truth, 1996), 23–33.

8. See Appendix 1: The Ecumenical Creeds.

not only a true human body but also a "reasonable [rational] soul" is essential, for it is the term our fathers in the early church used in their battles over the true humanity of Christ. One such battle, the controversy with Apollinarius, was eventually settled at the third ecumenical Council in Ephesus in 431. This council affirmed that Jesus was one person with two full and complete natures. Apollinarius (310–390) was bishop of Laodicea and a great defender of the Christian faith as defined by the Nicene Creed. He erred in saying that humans are made up of three parts: a body, an animal soul (*anima animans*, which all animals have), and a rational soul (*anima rationalis*, a rational soul that differentiates humans from animals) and that in Jesus Christ, the eternal Word (Logos) took the place of the human spirit (*anima rationalis*) (fig. 1).

Animals	**Ordinary Human**	**Jesus Christ**
	Rational Soul	Word
Animal Soul	Animal Soul	Animal Soul
Body	Body	Body

FIGURE 1

Apollinarius taught this because he rightly feared that any doctrine separating the Son into the Son of God and the son of Mary imperiled our salvation and our worship. His reaction, though, was an extreme emphasis on the deity of Christ. He used phrases for Christ such as "the flesh-bearing God." Just as with modern-day expressions such as "all God in a bod," the implication was that Jesus Christ was not fully human.

In unity with the ancient church, orthodox Christians realize that Apollinarius's doctrine destroyed the true humanity of Christ. Apollinarius's Christ, like that of Eutyches, became a *tertium quid*, a "third thing." This fusion of the divine and human natures resulted in the glorification of Christ's flesh, for His divine attributes were substituted for human ones. The divine Word took the place of normal human psychology in Jesus Christ, who didn't derive His thoughts, emotions, and will from the human nature but from the divine. This also meant that Jesus's flesh was given life not by His humanity but by His deity. The result was that Jesus was no human at all, unable to "sympathize with our weaknesses" (Heb. 4:15). W. G. T. Shedd (1820–1894) said of Apollinarius's formulation, "If the rational part be subtracted from man, he becomes either an idiot or a brute."[9] The outcome, according to the church fathers Hilary of Poitiers (300–368), Gregory of Nazianzus, Basil of Caesarea (330–379), and Gregory of Nyssa (335–394) was that Jesus isn't our redeemer because He's not a true man.

The Synod of Alexandria (362) refuted Apollinarius's conception, saying Christ had a human soul, which they meant as the highest element of man in Apollinarius's scheme. The Definition of Chalcedon speaks against this serious heresy when it says that our Lord is "the same perfect in Godhead and also perfect in manhood; truly God and truly man, of a reasonable [rational] soul and body." Chalcedon affirms the divine and human natures, not a divine and a divine-human. The Definition also states that Christ is "consubstantial with us according to the Manhood."[10] He is of the same substance with us just as He is of the same substance as the Father.

---

9. Cited in Berkhof, *History of Christian Doctrines*, 103.
10. See Appendix 1: The Ecumenical Creeds.

Of the Virgin Mary

Another key to understanding the true humanity of our Lord is in the phrase in both the Apostles' and Nicene Creeds that Jesus was conceived by the Holy Spirit "of the Virgin Mary" (*ex Maria virgine*/*ek Marias tēs parthenou*).[11] This phrase comes directly from Scripture, which says that Jesus is "conceived in her" and born of her (Matt. 1:20–21; Gal. 4:4; cf. Gen. 3:15; Luke 2:7). What is its significance?

The Reformers of the sixteenth century defended the gospel of salvation through faith alone against the Roman Catholic Church. This is commonly understood. What's not so commonly understood is that they also had to defend the truly catholic doctrine of the incarnation against the Anabaptists (*ana*, "again," and *baptizō*, "baptize"; hence, "rebaptizers"). These radical groups rejected infant baptism, along with many other doctrines, as Roman Catholic error. Regarding the doctrine of the incarnation, many Anabaptists held to the views of heretical groups in the ancient church that rejected the true humanity of our Lord, such as the Docetists (Christ appeared to be human), the Gnostics (spirit is good, and flesh is evil), and the Modalists (God appears in various modes throughout history—as Father, as Son, and as Holy Spirit), whether ancient or modern. The Belgic Confession is one example of how Reformed theologians rejected the view of some Anabaptists that Christ didn't receive His

---

11. See the Augsburg Confession, art. 3; Scots Confession (1560), art. 6; Belgic Confession, art. 18; Heidelberg Catechism 35; Second Helvetic Confession (1566), chap. 11; Thirty-Nine Articles, art. 2; and Westminster Confession of Faith, chap. 8.2.

humanity from His mother, Mary. To do so it calls on an impressive string of biblical witnesses:

> We confess (in opposition to the heresy of the Anabaptists, who deny that Christ assumed human flesh of his mother) that Christ is become a partaker of the flesh and blood of the children [Heb. 2:14]; that he is a fruit of the loins of David after the flesh (Acts 2:30); made of the seed of David according to the flesh (Ps. 132:11; Rom. 1:3); a fruit of the womb of the Virgin Mary (Luke 1:42); made of a woman (Gal. 4:4); a branch of David (Jer. 33:15); a shoot of the root of Jesse (Isa. 11:1); sprung from the tribe of Judah (Heb. 7:14); descended from the Jews according to the flesh (Rom. 9:5); of the seed of Abraham, since he took on him the seed of Abraham (Gen. 22:18; 2 Sam. 7:12; Matt. 1:1; Gal. 3:16), and became like unto his brethren in all things, sin excepted (Heb. 2:17, 4:15); so that in truth he is our Immanuel, that is to say, God with us [Isa. 7:14; Matt. 1:23] (art. 18).[12]

The Anabaptists didn't deny that Christ was born of Mary or that He was fully God. They did deny, however, that He received His human nature from His earthly mother. Some Anabaptists compared Mary to a funnel, saying that the Son merely passed through her as a conduit to get to earth; hence, He didn't take on a human nature. Their reasoning sprang from a Gnostic error. Gnosticism was a teaching that threatened the church in its first three centuries. The basic premise of the Gnostics was that spirit was good and flesh was evil.

---

12. Schaff, *Creeds*, 3:403. On this list of biblical passages, see Hyde, *With Heart and Mouth*, 240.

The Son of Man: Christ's Human Nature

The material world was bad just because it was material. But historic Christians believe Jesus was born "of Mary," "of her substance" (Thirty-Nine Articles, 2; Westminster Confession of Faith 8.2).

The Belgic Confession agrees with Scripture in teaching that it's imperative for Jesus Christ to be a true man in order to save humanity from their sin. Since the curse of sin fell on humanity, the curse had to be reversed by a human. In its defense of the true humanity of Christ, the Belgic Confession uses the magnificent presentation of Hebrews 1–2 that the Son is great over angels in both His exaltation and humiliation and then ties this to the reality and necessity of the incarnation. The conclusion to this argument is in 2:10–18:

> For it was fitting for Him, for whom are all things and by whom are all things, in bringing many sons to glory, to make the captain of their salvation perfect through sufferings. For both He who sanctifies and those who are being sanctified are all of one, for which reason He is not ashamed to call them brethren, saying:
>
> > "I will declare Your name to My brethren;
> > In the midst of the assembly I will sing praise to You."
>
> And again:
>
> > "I will put My trust in Him."
>
> And again:
>
> > "Here am I and the children whom God has given Me."
>
> Inasmuch then as the children have partaken of flesh and blood, He Himself likewise shared in the same,

that through death He might destroy him who had the power of death, that is, the devil, and release those who through fear of death were all their lifetime subject to bondage. For indeed He does not give aid to angels, but He does give aid to the seed of Abraham. Therefore, in all things He had to be made like His brethren, that He might be a merciful and faithful High Priest in things pertaining to God, to make propitiation for the sins of the people. For in that He Himself has suffered, being tempted, He is able to aid those who are tempted.

To describe this humiliation, the writer uses phrases such as "made a little lower than the angels" (v. 9). The text says the incarnation "was fitting," or suitable, proper, or right for Him (v. 10) and that "He had" necessarily "to be made like His brethren" (v. 17). It was fitting for the Son to suffer for us as our Mediator; it was necessary for Him to suffer as a man, with a body and soul.

Note what Hebrews 2 says about the suitability and necessity of Christ's true humanity being received from His mother. In verse 11 the writer speaks of the link between Christ and us, literally saying that we "are all of one" (*ex henos pantes*), meaning that we have one origin. In verse 14 the writer says that since we as humans "have partaken of flesh and blood," "He Himself likewise shared in the same." The writer is saying that Christ shares a common humanity with us. Just as we received our humanity from our parents, so also Christ received His humanity from Mary, His only earthly parent. He didn't just appear to be a human, as the ancient heresy of Docetism said; He *was* a human in the full sense of the term. The phrase "flesh and blood" connotes that

He was a human being; He was a man. Hebrews 2:17 says also that Jesus shared with us in our humanity "in all things." He was as human as human can be.

One interesting question to ponder about the true humanity of Jesus is that since we confess He received His humanity from His mother, where did His Y chromosome come from? The Y chromosome is contributed by the father to produce a male baby. Was a part of the miracle of the holy conception and incarnation that Jesus received the Y chromosome immediately by the Holy Spirit? Or perhaps the miracle was that Mary contributed the Y chromosome contrary to ordinary means? Regardless, it's a wonderful miracle indeed.

Sinless Humanity

We confess the true humanity of Jesus, that He was like us in every way. The only difference is that He was conceived without the stain of original sin. One of the ways to approach this is by discussing whether or not Mary was a sinner or was sinless. After all, David clearly taught in Psalm 51, "In sin my mother conceived me" (v. 5). Yet the Roman Catholic Church teaches a doctrine of the immaculate conception of Mary. This was decreed and defined by Pope Pius IX in the document *Ineffabilis Deus* (1854), which says, "The most Blessed Virgin Mary was, from the first moment of her conception, by a singular grace and privilege of almighty God and by view of the merits of Jesus Christ, the Savior of the human race, preserved free from all stain of original sin."[13]

---

13. Cited in *Catechism of the Catholic Church* 491 (New York: Doubleday, 1994), 138.

If Mary was sinless, then Jesus could be born sinless. We believe, though, that Mary was sinful like the rest of humanity. Her praise of "God my Savior" (Luke 1:47) after the angel Gabriel told her of the child in her womb evidences that she knew herself to be a sinner. Why would she need a savior if she was sinless? Because of this, the question must be asked, If Jesus Christ was born of a sinful woman, how could He be born sinless? The answer is in what the gospel writers say about the conception and birth of our Lord:

> Now the birth of Jesus Christ was as follows: After His mother Mary was betrothed to Joseph, before they came together, she was found with child *of the Holy Spirit*.... But while [Joseph] thought about these things, behold, an angel of the Lord appeared to him in a dream, saying, "Joseph, son of David, do not be afraid to take to you Mary your wife, for that which is conceived in her is *of the Holy Spirit*." (Matt. 1:18, 20)

> And the angel answered and said to her, "*The Holy Spirit will come upon you*, and *the power of the Highest will overshadow you*; therefore, also, that Holy One who is to be born will be called the Son of God." (Luke 1:35)

What we learn in the Gospels is that the Son of God was "conceived in the womb of the blessed Virgin Mary, by the power of the Holy Ghost, without the means of man" (Belgic Confession, art. 18).[14] Heinrich Bullinger (1504–1575) stated it in a more literal way: "The eternal Son of the eternal God was made the Son of man...not from the coitus of a man...

---

14. Schaff, *Creeds*, 3:402–3.

but was most chastely conceived by the Holy Spirit" (Second Helvetic Confession, chap. 11).[15] This is how He was sinless—not because of Mary. Heidelberg Catechism 35 teaches this as well when it says that Jesus's conception was "by the operation of the Holy Ghost."[16] Also, other New Testament passages testify that Jesus "knew no sin" (2 Cor. 5:21; cf. Heb. 4:15; 9:14), describing Him as "holy, harmless, undefiled, separate from sinners" (Heb. 7:26); saying that He "committed no sin, nor was deceit found in His mouth" (1 Peter 2:22); and that "in Him there is no sin" (1 John 3:5). Thus, the church confessed in the Athanasian Creed that Jesus was not only "perfect God" but also "perfect man."

True Humanity Illustrated

The confession of Jesus Christ being truly human in every respect like us, with a body and a soul, is illustrated in the gospel narratives. We see in these stories of Jesus's life that He experienced all the emotions of human existence, including anger (e.g., Mark 3:5), disgust (e.g., Mark 8:12), and distress (e.g., John 12:27). He showed His ability to express human capacities such as affection, compassion (Mark 9:36–37), and sympathy (Heb. 4:15). Most touchingly, when His friend Lazarus lay in the tomb, Jesus wept (John 11:35). Thus, in the incarnation we confess that God became a true man. The father Theodore of Mopsuestia (350–428) said that Christ struggled as a true man with all the human passions, passing

---

15. This Reformation confession is the only one to my knowledge that affirms the perpetual virginity of Mary when it says the Son was "born of Mary, who was always a virgin" (*et natum ex Maria semper virgine*; chap. 11).

16. Schaff, *Creeds*, 3:319.

through a great conflict with many temptations and coming out of it all victoriously.[17]

One Will or Two?

In my discussion of the two natures of Christ, I mentioned the false teaching of Eutyches, who claimed that Christ's humanity was swallowed up by His divinity. This meant that Christ had only one nature. After he was condemned, his teaching resurfaced among a group called the Monophysites—that is, those who believed Christ had one (*mono*) nature (*phusis*). The continual presence of the Monophysites led the church to ask another mysterious, yet important question: Did Jesus Christ have one will or two? Did He have only a divine will (that swallowed up the human), or did He have both a human and a divine will, just as He had a human and a divine nature? A question that arises from this discussion is whether Christ could have been afraid of His sufferings and death. Obviously, in terms of His divine nature, He is eternal Son. As the eternal Son, He came to earth to save sinners. This is why He could pray, "I have glorified You on the earth. I have finished the work which You have given Me to do" (John 17:4). He and the Father had willed for Him to perform that work from all eternity. Hence, Jesus had a divine will.

Those in the ancient church who said this was the only will Christ had were the Monothelites, a group of the Monophysites. They were called this since they believed Jesus Christ had only one (*mono*) will (*thelema*). The official answer of the Christian church to the Monothelites on this question

---

17. Berkhof, *History of Christian Doctrines*, 104.

was given at the Council of Constantinople (680–681). Their answer is what true catholic Christians confess: our Lord has two wills that work in harmonious unity, and His human will is subject to His divine will. Constantinople said,

> We likewise declare that in him are two natural wills and two natural operations indivisibly, inconvertibly, inseparably, inconfusedly, according to the teaching of the holy Fathers. And these two natural wills are not contrary the one to the other (God forbid!) as the impious heretics assert, but his human will follows and that not as resisting and reluctant, but rather as subject to his divine and omnipotent will.... We glorify two natural operations indivisibly, immutably, inconfusedly, inseparably in the same our Lord Jesus Christ our true God, that is to say a divine operation and a human operation.... We recognize the miracles and the sufferings as of one and the same [person], but of one or of the other nature of which he is and in which he exists, as Cyril admirably says. Preserving therefore the inconfusedness and indivisibility, we make briefly this whole confession, believing our Lord Jesus Christ to be one of the Trinity and after the incarnation our true God, we say that his two natures shone forth in his one subsistence in which he both performed the miracles and endured the sufferings through the whole of his economic conversation, and that not in appearance only but in very deed, and this by reason of the difference of nature which must be recognized in the same Person, for although joined together yet each nature wills and does the things proper to it and that indivisibly and inconfusedly. Wherefore we confess two

wills and two operations, concurring most fitly in him for the salvation of the human race.[18]

Thus, historically orthodox Christians like me are Duothelites: we believe Jesus has two wills. Why? To answer that, go back to the question of whether Jesus could have experienced fear at His death. We have to think not merely of His eternal will and purpose to come to earth and save sinners. We also have to think of His experience while on earth. For example, the night before His crucifixion, He prayed in the garden of Gethsemane:

> "O My Father, if it is possible, let this cup pass from Me; *nevertheless, not as I will, but as You will.*"…
>
> Again, a second time, He went away and prayed, saying, "O My Father, *if this cup cannot pass away from Me unless I drink it, Your will be done.*"…
>
> So He left them, went away again, and prayed the third time, saying the same words. (Matt. 26:39, 42, 44)

Our Lord came with a will to do His Father's will, yet He also submitted His will to His Father's will in the face of death. What this means is that our Lord has two wills. He has a divine will, consistent with a divine nature. He has a human will, consistent with a human nature. In this way, again, we learn that our Lord was and is truly human that He might truly be our Savior.

---

18. Council of Constantinople, in *Nicene and Post-Nicene Fathers*, Second Series, ed. Philip Schaff and Henry Wace (1900; repr., Peabody, Mass: Hendrickson, 2004), 14:345–46.

The Necessity of the Incarnation

So if a human being is composed of a body and soul and both body and soul are affected by our sin nature, why was it necessary for Jesus Christ to have both a body and a soul? Belgic Confession, article 18, addresses this question: "For since the soul was lost as well as the body, it was necessary that He should take both upon Him, to save both." In this statement the Reformers followed the orthodox, catholic doctrine of Christ explained above. In doing so they drew on the famous phrase of Gregory of Nazianzus: "For that which He has not assumed He has not healed."[19] If Christ had only a body, your soul is lost forever; if He had only a soul, your body is lost forever. We need the Savior to be truly human so that we might gain salvation for both body and soul.

Another reason for the necessity of the incarnation is because of our human weakness and sin. Because God truly became a man, He's able to be "a merciful and faithful High Priest" (Heb. 2:17). In other words, He knows our struggles as a fellow human. Thus, as a priest like us, He can offer up the appropriate sacrifice for our sins. As the apostolic writer goes on to say, because He "has suffered, being tempted, He is able to aid those who are tempted" (v. 18). Jesus can come to our aid when we need Him. Jesus understands when we pray to Him during trial and temptation. This is why the writer to the Hebrews says, "For indeed He does not give aid to angels, but He does give aid to the seed of Abraham" (v. 16). Amazingly,

---

19. Gregory of Nazianzus, *Epistle 101: To Cledonius the Priest against Apollinarius*, in *Nicene and Post-Nicene Fathers*, Second Series, trans. Charles Gordon Brown and James Edward Swallow (1894; repr., Peabody, Mass.: Hendrickson, 2004), 7:440.

he says this about our Savior, who is both God and man; thus, God understands our temptations, our weaknesses, and our needs—because Christ does. His mercy and aid come to us as sympathy and empathy—sympathy because He understands our struggles, empathy because He has experienced them. In sum, "we do not have a High Priest who cannot sympathize with our weaknesses, but was in all points tempted as we are, yet without sin" (Heb. 4:15).

Because of our Lord's sympathy and empathy for us, His brothers, He can also be a faithful High Priest in praying for the "prayer requests" of His friends. Hebrews 7:25 makes one of the most beautiful statements in all of Scripture: "Therefore He is also able to save to the uttermost those who come to God through Him, since He always lives to make intercession for them." The purpose of our Lord's resurrection, ascension, and heavenly session at the right hand of God is to intercede for us. He is "a Minister of the sanctuary and of the true tabernacle which the Lord erected, and not man" (Heb. 8:2). Our greater High Priest (4:14), who offered a greater sacrifice (9:23) in order to inaugurate a greater covenant (8:6, 13), now ministers in the "greater and more perfect tabernacle" (9:11) for our benefit—"for us" (v. 24). We shouldn't think of His intercession as Him praying for things like we do, hoping we offer up just the right words at the right time to get God to listen to us. No, His presence at the right hand of God in the presence of the heavenly sanctuary *is* His intercession for us. Because His sacrifice is complete, His intercession is complete and perfect.

"What if God was one of us?" the singer asked. The Lord Jesus Christ was and remains truly human. The Lord assumed all the elements that make us human except sin. He has a body like ours. He has a soul like ours. He experienced the difficulties of life as we do. In the 2008 movie *The Dark Knight*, police lieutenant Jim Gordon tells his son the police need to hunt down Batman "because he's the hero Gotham deserves, but not the one it needs right now." As humans, we so often think of political, societal, and religious salvation in terms of *deserve*. If we're worthy enough, we'll get a good leader. If we work hard enough, we'll change society. If we do enough good works, God will be pleased with us. Unlike Batman, Jesus is the Savior we don't deserve because we've sinned against Him, and He's the one we need right now. As the Savior we need, fully God and fully man, He went to the cross to die for our sins so that we can then come to Him in times when we need sympathy.

Conclusion

In conclusion, the reality of Jesus Christ's humanity has been expressed in no better way than by the North African bishop and theologian Tertullian of Carthage. In his written polemics against the condemned heretic Marcion (85–160) and his followers, Tertullian graphically and powerfully taught the Lord's full humanity:

> Come now, beginning from the nativity itself, declaim against the uncleanness of the generative elements within the womb, the filthy concretion of fluid and blood, of the growth of the flesh for nine months long out of that very mire. Describe the womb as it enlarges from day to day, heavy, troublesome, restless even in sleep, changeful in its feelings of dislike and desire. Inveigh now likewise against the shame itself of a woman in travail which, however, ought rather to be honoured in consideration of

that peril, or to be held sacred in respect of (the mystery of) nature. Of course you are horrified also at the infant, which is shed into life with the embarrassments which accompany it from the womb; you likewise, of course, loathe it even after it is washed, when it is dressed out in its swaddling-clothes, graced with repeated anointing, smiled on with nurse's fawns.[20]

Tertullian's rhetoric was that Marcion's rejection of the true humanity of Christ led him to have contempt for the course of nature—the same way he had been born! In fact, if Marcion hated the humanity of Christ, Tertullian asked him, "after what fashion do you love anybody?" Despite Marcion's hatred, the incarnation shows the love of Christ for humanity:

Christ, at any rate, has loved even that man who was condensed in his mother's womb amidst all its uncleannesses, even that man who was brought into life out of the said womb, even that man who was nursed amidst the nurse's simpers. For his sake He came down (from heaven), for his sake He preached, for his sake "He humbled Himself even unto death—the death of the cross." He loved, of course, the being whom He redeemed at so great a cost.... Well, then, loving man He loved his nativity also, and his flesh as well. Nothing can be loved apart from that through which whatever exists has its existence.[21]

---

20. Tertullian, *On the Flesh of Christ*, chap. 4, in *Ante-Nicene Fathers*, trans. P. Holmes (1885; repr., Peabody, Mass.: Hendrickson, 2004), 3:524.

21. Tertullian, *On the Flesh of Christ*, chap. 4, 524.

The incarnation of the Son into a real human nature shows not only the love of Christ but also the true wisdom of God. Echoing Paul's words concerning the world's wisdom and God's foolishness (which in reality is God's wisdom and the world's foolishness), Tertullian said, "It is of course foolish, if we are to judge God by our own conceptions…. And yet, according to the world's wisdom, it is [easier] to believe that Jupiter became a bull or a swan, if we listen to Marcion, than that Christ really became a man."[22] Tertullian said, furthermore, that our wisdom is found in becoming foolish in the eyes of the world and by embracing the true wisdom of God: "The Son of God was crucified; I am not ashamed because men must needs be ashamed of it. And the Son of God died; it is by all means to be believed, because it is absurd. And He was buried, and rose again; the fact is certain, because it is impossible."[23] This impossibility is that God *is* one of us.

> Though circled by the hosts on high,
> He deigned to cast a pitying eye
> Upon his helpless creature;
> The whole creation's Head and Lord,
> By highest seraphim adored,
> Assumed our very nature.
> Jesus, grant us,
> Through Thy merit to inherit Thy salvation;
> Hear, O hear our supplication.[24]

---

22. Tertullian, *On the Flesh of Christ*, chap. 4, 524–25.

23. Tertullian, *On the Flesh of Christ*, chap. 5, 525.

24. Philip Nicolai, "How Bright Appears the Morning Star," in *Psalter Hymnal*, #336.

FIVE

The God-Man: Christ's Single Person

> I have glorified You on the earth. I have finished the work which You have given Me to do. And now, O Father, glorify Me together with Yourself, with the glory which I had with You before the world was.
>
> —JOHN 17:4–5

If we confess that the Son of God came to earth from heaven, that He took for Himself a human nature, and that with each nature He retains what's proper to it, then it goes without saying that we're on the precipice of a profound mystery. That Christ has two distinct natures doesn't mean they were mixed into being one nature in one person (Eutychianism); changed into being a new nature in one person (Apollinarianism); or, as we will learn in this chapter, that they were so separate that Christ has two natures in two persons. This is what Christ isn't. What He is, as limited as our vocabulary may be, is two properly distinct natures united in one person. After all, in the Gospels Jesus speaks in the first person singular—"I" and "My"—not "We" and "Ours."

The sixteenth-century Reformed confessions again helpfully express this union of Christ's two natures in His one person. Belgic Confession, article 19, says,

> But these two natures are so closely united in one person, that they were not separated even by his death. Therefore that which he, when dying, commended into the hands of his Father, was a real human spirit, departing from his body. But in the mean time the divine nature always remained united with the human, even when he lay in the grave; and the Godhead did not cease to be in him, any more than it did when he was an infant, though it did not so clearly manifest itself for a while.[1]

To help us grasp just how real this union is between His two natures in one person, the Confession gives a few illustrations. When He died, He commended His human spirit to His Father. But it was not as if His divine nature, which Jesus said was spirit (John 4:24), ascended to heaven while His human nature descended into the grave. In fact, while His human spirit was with His Father in heaven and His human body lay in the tomb of Joseph of Arimathea, "the divine nature always remained united with the human," although it was separated by the curse of death. The Confession speaks of this union of divine and human in the person of Christ by illustrating it from the infancy of the Lord. The divine nature didn't manifest itself until later in His life during His ministry—for example, in His healings. Yet the divine nature was united to the human even at conception, at birth, and during

---

1. Schaff, *Creeds*, 3:404–5.

childhood. As we'll see, this means we can say in Christ, God was born; in Christ, God nursed at His mother's breast; in Christ, God had His diapers changed; and in Christ, God played in the streets with His friends. So amazing is the unity of the person of the Lord Jesus Christ!

The Error of Dividing the Natures

Those who confess the union of the two natures in one person stand with the church against the heresy known as Nestorianism. Nestorius (381–452) became bishop of Constantinople in 428, just before the Council of Ephesus (431). He was an eloquent and orthodox preacher. His trouble began, though, with the phrase *theotokos* ("bearer of God" or "mother of God"). The church had called Mary *theotokos* in the context of the Arian controversy about whether the Son of God was eternal God. *Theotokos* was not used as a title of worship for Mary but to make a statement about the child she bore. The focus was not that Christ received His divine nature from Mary but that the child in Mary's womb was fully divine; thus, Jesus is God. For this reason, all orthodox Christian writers agree with the Reformed theologian Wollebius, who said, "Mary ought not only be called mother of Christ (as the Nestorians admitted), but also the mother of God."[2]

Thinking this term would lead to confusion, Nestorius called Mary *christotokos* ("bearer of Christ" or "mother of Christ"). By this term, he sought to establish that Mary didn't give birth to the divine Logos but to the man Jesus, whose human nature was united with the eternal Son. He preached

---

2. Wollebius, *Compendium Theologiae Christianae*, 94.

provocative sermons to this effect, saying a woman couldn't carry the deity for nine months in her womb, that the deity could hardly be wrapped in diapers, and that God couldn't have suffered, died, and been buried. Properly speaking of deity, this is true; but of Christ we're speaking of the Son-in-flesh.

The Council of Ephesus charged Nestorius with teaching that Jesus was two persons—one divine and the other human. In modern terms, this would make Jesus a schizophrenic or imply that His divine and human natures were somehow united like Siamese twins. Nestorius's overemphasis was a radical duality of Christ's two natures (fig. 2).

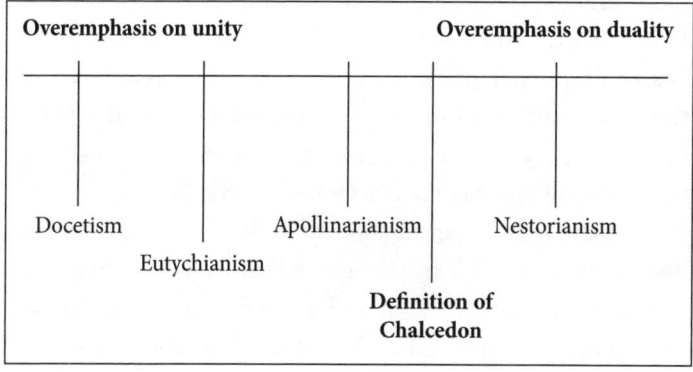

FIGURE 2

Reformed churches historically join orthodox Christian theologians on this issue. As we've seen, the second person of the Holy Trinity—the Son—took to Himself, or assumed, a human nature, not a human person. The human nature of Christ never had a separate existence apart from the union that occurred in the incarnation. The eternal Son added to

Himself the nature of humanity—body and soul—in order to be the Savior of humanity.

In Nestorius's view, the eternal Son of God came to live in the man Jesus as though he were a temple. We can illustrate Nestorius's teaching by considering what happens when oil is mixed with water in one container. They don't unite; the oil remains distinctly oil, and the water remains distinctly water. There's no true union, only division and distinction. The fathers at Chalcedon had Nestorius's teaching in mind when they confessed "one and the same Son," who is "to be acknowledged in two natures…indivisibly, inseparably…not parted or divided into two persons, but one and the same Son, and only begotten, God the Word, the Lord Jesus Christ."[3] This one Son was born of Mary, *theotokos*, "the bearer or mother of God." The Athanasian Creed also says this: "Who although he be God and Man; yet he is not two, but one Christ. For as the reasonable soul and flesh is one man: so God and Man is one Christ" (§§34, 37).[4]

Is there any danger in confessing that Christ is really two distinct *persons*? Yes. The danger is that He would have been two saviors: a divine savior and a human savior. In the end, He would be no savior at all. We wouldn't be able to approach Him in prayer as the "divine" savior because He would be holy God while we're lowly sinners. If we approached the "human" savior, we would have no confidence that anything He did would be effectual since He wouldn't be God at the same time. Christ wouldn't be the "one Mediator" Paul wrote

---

3. See Appendix 1: The Ecumenical Creeds.
4. See Appendix 1: The Ecumenical Creeds.

of (1 Tim. 2:5) between a holy God and sinful humanity. The same chasm that exists between this holy God and us sinners would exist between the divine and human persons.

The Relationship of These Two Natures

In the early church, more controversy arose concerning how the qualities proper to each of Jesus's natures related to each other. In other words, the Son is divine, so how do we speak of Him on earth eating, drinking, and sleeping? Jesus is human, so how do we speak of Him walking on water, healing the sick, and forgiving sins? Early church theologians spoke of the "communication of proper qualities" (*communicatio idiomatum*); that is, how these natures not only relate but how we can speak of them in relation to the one person of Christ at the same time. This was given basic expression by Origen in the mid-third century:

> Therefore deservedly is it [the divine nature] also called, along with the flesh which it had assumed, the Son of God, and the Power of God, the Christ, and the Wisdom of God, either because it was wholly in the Son of God, or because it received the Son of God wholly into itself.... Again, the Son of God, through whom all things were created, is named Jesus Christ and the Son of man. For the Son of God also is said to have died—in reference…to that nature which could admit of death; and He is called the Son of man, who is announced as about to come in the glory of God the Father, with the holy angels.... For this reason, throughout the whole of Scripture, not only is the divine nature spoken of

in human words, but the human nature is adorned by appellations of divine dignity.[5]

At the time of the Reformation, two viewpoints prevailed concerning the interpretation of the *communicatio idiomatum* among Protestants. On the one hand, the Lutheran Protestant view is that the two natures of Christ actually share their distinctive traits and that the properties of the divine nature can be exchanged with the human nature. On the other hand, the Reformed Protestant viewpoint is that there's a communion of both the divine and human natures in the one person of Christ, while each nature retains its distinctness (fig. 3):

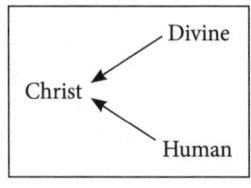

FIGURE 3

As a Reformed theologian, I maintain that in the one person of Christ there are two natures, not just as a manner of speaking but because it's the truth about the reality of the incarnation. Because of this mysterious union, whatever is done peculiarly by either the divine or human natures of Christ can be communicated verbally of the one person of Christ. This is expressed in two ways in Scripture.

---

5. Origen, *De Principiis* 2.6.3.

What Is Said of the Human Nature Is Said of the Person
First, we read statements affirming a truth about the human nature being attributed to the person of Christ. For example, the person of the Son is said not to know the day or hour of His return to the earth (Mark 13:32). How is that possible? Because of the limitations of the *human* nature. Therefore, properly speaking, the human nature of Christ died on the cross. Nevertheless, because of the union of the two natures in the one person, the apostle Paul can say that "the Lord of glory" was crucified and died on the cross (1 Cor. 2:8). Also, Paul speaks to elders and calls them to oversee "the church of God which [God] purchased with *His* own blood" (Acts 20:28). Therefore, another Reformed confession, the Canons of Dort (1618–1619), applied this to the doctrines associated with the death of the Lord:

> The *death of the Son of God* is the only and most perfect sacrifice and satisfaction for sin; is of infinite worth and value, abundantly sufficient to expiate the sins of the whole world. (II, 3)

> This death derives its infinite value and dignity from these considerations; because *the person* who submitted to it was *not only really man* and perfectly holy, but *also the only-begotten Son* of God, of the same eternal and infinite essence with the Father and Holy Spirit, which qualifications were necessary to constitute him a Saviour for us; and because it was attended with a sense of the wrath and curse of God due to us for sin. (II, 4)[6]

---

6. Schaff, *Creeds*, 3:586.

In other words, according to the Canons, the death of Jesus's human nature has infinite value because as it was united to the Son in the person, it was the God-man who died on the cross. Although the human nature died, its value is attributed to the person.

What Is Said of the Divine Nature Is Said of the Person

In terms of the *communicatio idiomatum*, we also read statements in Scripture affirming a truth about the divine nature being attributed to the person of Christ. For example, Christ calls Himself the "I AM" of Exodus 3:14 (John 8:58). Since Christ's divine nature is of the same substance as the Father, the person of Christ can be said to be eternal and immutable and cannot die. As well, the Son in whom we have redemption is "before all things" (Col. 1:17). In our worship we worship the person of Christ on the basis of the divine nature of Christ.[7] The reason for saying this is that for us to worship any man, albeit a perfect man such as our Lord, would be idolatry: "You shall worship the LORD your God, and Him only you shall serve" (Matt. 4:10). Yet because of the union of the two natures, we worship the one person of Christ, the God-man.[8]

We sometimes read of divine attributes being ascribed to the person of Christ when the person is designated by a human title. Thus, it is the Son of Man who ascends into

---

7. Herman Bavinck, *Reformed Dogmatics*, ed. John Bolt, trans. John Vriend (Grand Rapids: Baker Academic, 2006), 3:316–19; cf. Bavinck, *Our Reasonable Faith*, 328.

8. See Bavinck, *Reformed Dogmatics*, 3:318, for the list of Reformed theologians on both sides of this knotty theological issue—whether we worship Christ on the basis of His divinity (e.g., Johannes Maccovius) or on the basis of His divinity *and* His being the Mediator (e.g., William Ames).

heaven and descends from heaven (John 3:13; 6:62). Also, Paul says that Christ, who descended from the line of the patriarchs, "is over all, the eternally blessed God" (Rom. 9:5).

In summary, what we say about each nature, whether the divine or the human, we can say about the one person of the Lord Jesus Christ. Since the divine nature is eternal, we can speak of the person of Christ being eternal. Since the human nature was a real human nature that died, we can speak of the person of Christ dying on the cross. Again, this is in the realm of deep mystery that our words can't fully express. God can't die, yet it was the second person of the Holy Trinity, the incarnate Son, who died. This is why the "four fences of Chalcedon" are so wise in their expressing the distinction and union of Christ's natures negatively: without confusion (*asugchutōs*), without change (*atreptōs*), without division (*adiairetōs*), without separation (*achōristōs*).[9]

Divinity beyond Humanity

I've established that our Lord has two distinct natures united in a single person. Yet despite this union, the divine nature of Christ cannot be contained by the human nature. This belief is what is called the *extra Calvinisticum*, which is Latin for "the Calvinistic extra [outside]." Sixteenth- and seventeenth-century Lutheran theologians used this term in a pejorative, polemical sense to describe the Reformed teaching. The Reformed said the divine nature of Christ was "incomprehensible and everywhere present" and therefore wasn't constrained and bound by His humanity but is "indeed beyond the bounds of

---

9. See Appendix 1: The Ecumenical Creeds.

the manhood" (Heidelberg Catechism 48). All the while, the divine and human natures of Christ were united "indivisibly" and "inseparably" (Definition of Chalcedon). Calvinists believe that even while in the state of humiliation before His ascension, the Son of God filled the universe and upheld all things as God; hence, the Calvinistic *extra*. Calvin himself expressed this: "Here is something marvelous: the Son of God descended from heaven in such a way that, without leaving heaven, he willed to be borne in the virgin's womb, to go about the earth, and to hang upon the cross; yet he continuously filled the world even as he had done from the beginning."[10]

More recently, Michael Horton wrote of the *extra*: "Even as he lay in Mary's womb for nine months and walked along the shores of Galilee or Jerusalem, he continued to fill the heavens and the earth according to his omnipresent and omnipotent Godhead."[11] Thus, Reformed theologians coined the saying "The whole Christ (*totus Christus*) is everywhere, but not the whole of Christ (*totem Christi*)."[12] This means we can speak of the person of Christ being everywhere because He's divine; yet because He has a human nature, His humanity is finite and limited to one place. Another way the Reformed theologians spoke of this truth was to use the Latin phrase *finitum non capax infinitum*, which means "the finite [human nature] cannot contain the infinite [divine nature]." If the

---

10. Calvin, *Institutes*, 2.13.4.

11. Horton, *We Believe*, 81. In a more recent work, Horton said, "Even as he nursed at Mary's breast, the Son of God continued to fill the cosmos." *Lord and Servant: A Covenant Christology* (Louisville: Westminster John Knox, 2005), 163.

12. Wollebius, *Compendium Theologiae Christianae*, 92. See also Muller, *Dictionary*, 111, 305.

divine nature could be contained, it would cease to be divine; if the human nature could contain the divine, it wouldn't be human—in fact, it would be divine.

We find the Calvinistic extra in Scripture in general truths such as God being omnipresent (He's everywhere) and immense (He fills everything). We see it specifically in Scripture texts in which the apostle writes of the "Word made flesh" (John 1:14) and Christ being "in the bosom of the Father" (v. 18). Although this verse could be referring to Christ's ascension, its context is the incarnation. While incarnate as the "Word made flesh," "the only begotten Son" (John 1:18) is (present tense) in the Father's bosom.[13]

This fact of the eternal, infinite, immense, and omnipresent deity of the Son being outside the bounds and limits of the humanity of Christ was expressed masterfully by the fourth-century church father Athanasius. It's a lengthy quote, so I'll break it down: "For He was not, as might be imagined, circumscribed [contained] in the body, nor, while present in the body, was He absent elsewhere." That's the doctrine in a nutshell. While on earth, the Son of God wasn't contained within Jesus's humanity nor was He absent from heaven.

---

13. A more difficult text to establish this is John 3:13, which in the ASV and KJV says, "And no one hath ascended into heaven, but he that descended out of heaven, even the Son of man, *who* [*which*, KJV] *is in heaven*." The textual evidence for this phrase has led all modern English versions to delete it because what are considered the oldest manuscripts do not contain it. Even competent yet critical scholars such as Raymond Brown admit, "The textual evidence is not strong, but the phrase is so difficult that it may well have been omitted in the majority of manuscripts to avoid a difficulty.... The Son in John remains close to the Father even when he is on earth (1:18)." *Gospel according to John I–XII*, 133.

Athanasius continued: "Nor, while He moved the [human] body, was the universe left void of His working and Providence. But, thing most [marvelous], Word as He was, so far from being contained by anything, He rather contained all things Himself." While incarnate He still upheld all things (Heb. 1:3) and was working in all things (John 5:17). Of His providence Athanasius said,

> And just as while present in the whole of Creation, He is at once distinct in being from the universe, and present in all things by His own power,—giving order to all things, and over all and in all revealing His own providence, and giving life to each thing and all things, including the whole without being included, but being in His own Father alone wholly and in every respect.... Thus, even while present in a human body and Himself quickening it, He was, without inconsistency, quickening the universe as well, and was in every process of nature, and was outside the whole, and while known from the body by His works, He was none the less manifest from the working of the universe as well.

He was within the creation yet transcended it! While He gave life to His own human body He gave life to the universe. Then Athanasius gave a few summary statements:

> The Word of God in His man's nature...was not bound to His body, but rather was Himself wielding it, so that He was not only in it, but was actually in everything, and while external to the universe, abode in His Father only.... And this was the wonderful thing that He was at

once walking as man, and as the Word was quickening all things, and as the Son was dwelling with His Father.[14]

The Son-in-flesh walked the shores of Galilee yet fellowshipped with His Father in eternity.

Conclusion

Although having two distinct and different natures, the Lord Jesus Christ is one person in which those natures are united. What He did for us as both God and man, therefore, He did for us in the one work of the one Savior. The meaning of all this for us who can't even comprehend such a complex doctrine is that by faith in Him we may simply approach the Savior. Why? He's both willing and able to lead us into the presence of God to have fellowship with our Creator.

> King of kings, yet born of Mary,
> As of old on earth he stood,
> Lord of lords, in human vesture,
> In the body and the blood,
> He will give to all the faithful
> His own self for heav'nly food.[15]

---

14. Athanasius, *On the Incarnation*, 4:45.

15. Liturgy of St. James, fifth century, "Let All Mortal Flesh Keep Silence," in *Trinity Hymnal*, rev. ed. (Norcross, Ga.: Great Commission Publications, 1990), 193.

SIX

The Importance of This Mysterious Doctrine

And this is eternal life, that they may know You, the
only true God, and Jesus Christ whom You have sent.
—JOHN 17:3

Former professor of Christian apologetics at Westminster Theological Seminary in Philadelphia, Cornelius Van Til (1895–1987) once said regarding Jesus Christ's resurrection: "A man has risen from the grave? What a surprising occurrence! Send it to Ripley! Believe it or not!"[1] His point was that if we simply take the resurrection of the Lord as a "brute fact," a mere historical occurrence that is there for all to see, then the resurrection has no significance and implication for anyone's faith and life. Saul of Tarsus was a Jewish rabbi who actively sought to persecute Christians and stamp out the church's witness. Then he was converted and became known by his Roman name: Paul. We believe with him that Christ was not merely "raised again" but that He was raised "*for our*

---

1. Cited in Robert B. Strimple, *Christ Our Savior*, ST602 Doctrine of Christ Syllabus (Westminster Seminary California, Spring 2001), 21, https://wscal.edu/media/docs/Course-2-Syllabus.pdf.

justification" (Rom. 4:25 KJV). If He is not risen, "then our preaching is empty and your faith is also empty" (1 Cor. 15:14) and "you are still in your sins!" (v. 17).

The same is true of the incarnation of the Son of God in human flesh, soul, and history. If the Son of God wasn't incarnate, then our faith is futile, we're still in our sins, and we're of all men most to be pitied (1 Cor. 15:19). Even if He were incarnate simply as a spectacle for people to see or as a way for Him to do some investigatory journalism about His creation, it would mean nothing. It would be a brute fact.

The fact, though, is that God was and is "one of us." Because of this, He had a face, and seeing it, whether in person as the apostles or by faith through the means of His word preached, read, or even discussed in this book, means that we must believe in Him. On this side of faith, believing "in things like heaven and in Jesus and the saints and all the prophets," as the singer puts it, is not so bad after all.

Just how important is this mysterious doctrine, then? What does it mean for the question of faith? What does it mean for what we are to worship? What does it mean for your life and the lives of your immediate family—your spouse and your children? What does it mean for our churches and for our pastors' preaching? We need to explore these and other avenues of application in this chapter.

Apprehension, Not Comprehension

The incarnation of the Son demands your response of faith and trust. Jesus Himself said this to Nicodemus:

> For God so loved the world that He gave His only begotten Son, that whoever believes in Him should not perish

but have everlasting life. For God did not send His Son into the world to condemn the world, but that the world through Him might be saved.

He who believes in Him is not condemned; but he who does not believe is condemned already, because he has not believed in the name of the only begotten Son of God. (John 3:16–18)

Although we can't comprehend these mysterious doctrines of the incarnation of the eternal Son into temporal time and humanity or the hypostatic union of the two natures, we must apprehend their meaning by faith.[2] This is what Jesus spoke plainly when He said in His immense, infinite, and eternal love, God "gave" His only Son to the world. We'll never be able to grasp what the mysteries of Christ are all about, but we're still to confess them as true. As the Athanasian Creed says, "Furthermore it is necessary to everlasting salvation: that he also believe rightly [faithfully] the incarnation of our Lord Jesus Christ…. This is the Catholic Faith: which except a man believe faithfully [truly and firmly], he can not be saved" (§§29, 44).[3] We must believe as an act of humility before the Lord and His word. Herman Bavinck so eloquently confessed this:

> All those expressions and statements which are employed in the confession of the church and in the language of theology are not designed to explain the mystery which in this matter confronts it, but rather to maintain it pure and unviolated over against those who would weaken or

---

2. Berkhof, *Systematic Theology*, 315.
3. See Appendix 1: The Ecumenical Creeds.

deny it. The incarnation of the Word is not a problem which we must solve, or can solve, but a wonderful fact, rather, which we gratefully confess in such a way as God Himself presents it to us in His Word.[4]

We apprehend by faith alone the mystery of the Lord for the purpose of appropriating to ourselves the benefits that He won for us in His incarnation, life, death, and resurrection. To cite John Owen again:

> We speak of these things in a poor, low, broken manner,—we teach them as they are revealed in the Scripture,—we labour by faith to adhere unto them as revealed; but when we come into a steady, direct view and consideration of the thing itself, our minds fail, our hearts tremble, and we can find no rest but in a holy admiration of what we cannot comprehend. Here we are at a loss, and know that we shall be so whilst we are in this world; but all the ineffable fruits and benefits of this truth are communicated unto them that do believe.[5]

With the church fathers at Chalcedon, we confess that Christ's two natures are not confused or changed (against Eutyches/Monophysites) or divided or separated (against Nestorius). Jesus Christ is both consubstantial with His Father according to His divine nature and thus has conquered death and is consubstantial with us according to His human nature, with a true human body and rational soul (against Apollinarius). All this is necessary for us to know the One who lived in our place, died in our place, and rose again in our place.

---

4. Bavinck, *Our Reasonable Faith*, 322.
5. Owen, *Meditations and Discourses on the Glory of Christ*, in *Works*, 1:330.

Benefit of the Virgin Birth

The important doctrines of God with us and the virgin birth of our Lord are beneficial to us. This benefit was simply expressed by the Heidelberg Catechism, which asks, "What benefit dost thou receive from the holy conception and birth of Christ?" It answers: "That he is our Mediator, and with his innocence and perfect holiness covers, in the sight of God, my sin wherein I was conceived" (36).[6] As will be explained in greater detail below, we need a mediator who is both divine and human at the same time. As a human Mediator, our Lord was innocent and holy, not having original sin like us. The benefit of this is that we who are born in sin might receive a new birth in righteousness.

Mediator of the Covenant

The Belgic Confession concludes with a statement dealing with the importance of confessing the two natures of Christ: "Wherefore we confess that he is VERY GOD and VERY Man: very God by his power to conquer death, and very man that he might die for us according to the infirmity of His flesh" (art. 19).[7] As those dead in our own sins who stand before a holy God, we need a mediator to come to our level and lead us to God so that we might have a covenant relationship with Him not only as almighty God but also as a heavenly Father.

God the Father's relationship with His people throughout Scripture is described as a covenant—that is, a commitment. Since there are two sides to every covenant and since we can't

---

6. Schaff, *Creeds*, 3:319.
7. Schaff, *Creeds*, 3:405.

enter into a covenant with God in our sinful condition, God gave His Son to be a Mediator between Himself and us. The Westminster Confession of Faith so vividly and accurately expresses this truth when it says, "The distance between God and the creature is so great that although reasonable creatures do owe obedience unto him as their Creator, yet they could never have any fruition of Him as their blessedness and reward but by some voluntary condescension on God's part, which he hath been pleased to express by way of covenant" (7.1).[8]

As a "go between," this mediator must be both God, to represent God in the commitment, and man, to represent people in the commitment. This is wonderfully confessed in questions 12–19 of the Heidelberg Catechism. There we learn that because of our sins we need a human mediator to pay for them. Because of the infinite weight of God's justice against our sins, we need a divine Savior who'll be able to bear the weight of the punishment that is due to us. This Mediator is Jesus Christ, who is true God and true man.

Why We Need a Human Savior

The Heidelberg Catechism teaches in question 12 that since we have sinned against God, His justice requires payment. Questions 13–16 establish that since justice requires that the same human nature that sinned should also pay for sin, we need a human Savior. We can't make this payment (Q. 13), and neither can any other person or creature in our place since God will not punish any other creature for the sin we committed (Q. 14). Questions 12, 14, and 16 explain that since

---

8. Schaff, *Creeds*, 3:616.

it was man, in Adam, who was required to fulfill all righteousness in order to please God in the beginning, we need to satisfy for all our sins past, present, and future. Therefore, since we can't pay for our own sins, can't perfectly obey God, and can't satisfy for every one of our sins, we need another in our place. This Mediator must have a true human body and soul yet be without sin (Heb. 2:10–18; 4:15; 5:7–10).

Why We Need a Divine Savior

At the same time, the Scriptures clearly teach that no man, however holy and perfect he may be, can save us. There's only one Savior, and He will not give His glory to another (Isa. 43:11; Jer. 17:5–8; Hos. 13:4). Since Adam's sin was against an infinite God, an infinite satisfaction is required. Furthermore, since God's wrath is an infinite wrath, His wrath against sin is greater than any human can bear; therefore, we need a Savior who is also true God (Heidelberg Catechism 17). Machen powerfully stated, "Let us not deceive ourselves; a Jewish teacher of the first century can never satisfy the longing of our souls."[9] No mere man, however holy, can bring us into fellowship with God.

What is amazing in Scripture is that this is the case because God not only desired to give us grace that met our crimes against Him but that His grace would "super-abound" (*hupereperisseusen*) beyond our sins (Rom. 5:15–21). Only an infinite Savior could bring us an infinite grace. Had Christ not possessed the two natures of divinity and humanity in His one person, we would be without salvation.

---

9. Machen, *Christianity and Liberalism*, 41.

This is why Wollebius eloquently praised this most marvelous plan for our redemption in the midst of detailing the intricacies of Christian theology:

> Now by whose suffering could the crime against the infinite majesty be expiated, except him who was also infinite? By whose intercession could the wrath of God be turned aside, except his who was the most beloved Son of the Father? By whose power could Satan and all the power of darkness be vanquished, except his who is more powerful than all devils? And finally, who could overcome death except he who has power over death (Heb. 2:15)?… But who was able to give us righteousness except he who is righteous? Who could better make us sons of God than he who is naturally the Son of God? Who could more rightfully restore us to the image of God than he who is the image of the invisible God? Who could more surely confer the gifts of the Holy Spirit than he who proceeds from him? Finally, who could give eternal life but he who is life itself (John 1:4)?[10]

Was it necessary for the church fathers and the Reformers to defend the doctrine of the two natures in the one person of Christ? Given what was at stake, it certainly was necessary—despite the consequences. It remains necessary today to defend all that God has revealed in His word for the salvation of sinners.

---

10. Wollebius, *Compendium Theologiae Christianae*, 88.

Knowing Christ

Traditionally, from the time of the great scholastic theologians of the High Middle Ages, theologians have discussed Jesus Christ in terms of His person and work. It's because of who He is (His person) and what He did (His work) that we by faith alone are in a covenant relationship with God as Creator and Father. Christ's person and work are a unity. Without the person, there's no work, and the work is meaningless without the person accomplishing it. Although they gave us this helpful distinction, many medieval theologians focused so much on the discussion of the two natures of Christ that they neglected a mature biblical-theological discussion of the work of Christ for His people's benefit. Immersed in the mystery of the hypostatic union, they ended up asking overly philosophical questions about Christ.

The Reformers didn't react against this classic theological distinction or the doctrine of the hypostatic union, but against overly speculative theology and preaching that had no comforting benefit for the ordinary person. They followed the clear teaching of the Holy Scriptures in which these two categories aren't spoken of in abstract terms, separated from one another. Christ's person gives meaning and purpose to His work for us, and His work is grounded in who He is, His person (e.g., Col. 1:15–23; cf. Phil. 2:6–8; Heb. 1:2–3, 6, 8; 2:9–17). Christ's work has significance for us because of who He is. As Paul says in 2 Corinthians 8:9, Christ's poverty in the incarnation is important for us because by His becoming poor we have become rich in spiritual terms.

This relationship between Christ's person and work was expressed by Martin Luther's protégé Philip Melanchthon

(1497–1560), who said, "To acknowledge Christ is to acknowledge His benefits, not as is sometimes taught to behold His nature or the modes of His incarnation."[11] Martin Luther (1483–1546) said, "Christ is not called Christ because He has two natures; what is that to me? But he bears this glorious and comforting name from the office and work which he took upon himself. That he is by nature both God and man belongs to himself, but my comfort and benefit is that he used his office on my behalf, and poured out his love and became my Savior and Redeemer."[12] Therefore, both Luther and Melanchthon said that we come to know Christ not through contemplating His metaphysical nature but through apprehending who He is and what He did for us in His redemptive work.

We shouldn't take up this study of the person of Christ, which we call Christology, as an interesting intellectual exercise. We must not be involved with Christ as mere spectators or abstract questioners but must personally be involved in studying who He is and what He did because He is the one who will affect our lives for eternity as our Savior. This is why pastor-theologian John Calvin said, "The object of theology is not knowledge of God as He is in Himself, but rather the object of theology is the knowledge of God as He is for us."[13] We must not be interested so much in who Jesus is as an abstract person or idea but in what He did for us as Himself. We come to know in a tangible, concrete way that Jesus Christ is our divine-human Savior in this covenant relationship as it

---

11. Philip Melanchthon, *Loci Communes*, as quoted in Berkouwer, *Person of Christ*, 102.

12. Quoted in Berkouwer, *Person of Christ*, 103.

13. Calvin, *Institutes*, 1.2.2; 1.10.2.

is renewed with us every Lord's Day through the preaching of the word and celebration of the sacraments of baptism and the Lord's Supper.

In coming to know the God-man and His mighty work for us, we're granted by God a bold faith. In his Small Catechism explanation of the section of the Apostles' Creed that professes faith in Jesus Christ, Martin Luther said, "What does this mean? Answer: I believe that Jesus Christ, true God, begotten of the Father from eternity, and also true man, born of the Virgin Mary, is my Lord.... This is most certainly true."[14]

Knowing the Father

In coming to know Christ as our Mediator, we come to know God the Father. The apostle John tells us that while only the Son has ever seen and been with the Father from all eternity, the Son of God has come for the purpose of making this invisible and unknown Father visible in the face of Christ and through His words and works (John 1:18). This is why Jesus responded so mysteriously yet clearly to a request from His disciple Philip, who asked Jesus to show them the Father: "Have I been with you so long, and yet you have not known Me, Philip? He who has seen Me has seen the Father; so how can you say, 'Show us the Father'? Do you not believe that I am in the Father, and the Father in Me? The words that I speak to you I do not speak on My own authority; but the Father who dwells in Me does the works" (John 14:9–10).

The great defender of the faith Athanasius saw this truth as the purpose of the Lord's incarnation:

---

14. Small Catechism, in *Martin Luther's Basic Theological Writings*, ed. Timothy F. Lull (Minneapolis: Fortress, 1989), 480.

> For seeing that men, having rejected the contemplation of God, and with their eyes downward, as though sunk in the deep, were seeking about for God in nature and in the world of sense, feigning gods for themselves of mortal men and demons; to this end the loving and general Saviour of all, the Word of God, takes to Himself a body, and as Man walks among men and meets the senses of all men half-way, to the end, I say, that they who think that God is corporeal may from what the Lord effects by His body perceive the truth, and through Him recognize the Father.[15]

We looked for God in what we could see because God was unseen; therefore, the Son became visible and tangible to direct the eyes of men to Him and thereby upward to the Father who dwells in heaven.

Renewal of the Image of God

The Son's incarnation begins to restore us, for the story of Scripture is that of God making humanity in His image. In the garden of Eden, Adam "vitiated and almost blotted out" that image by the instigation of the devil.[16] Yet in grace, the Son of God came to earth as the second Adam (Rom. 5:14; 1 Cor. 15:45) to "destroy the works of the devil" (1 John 3:8) and to re-create His people in the image of God. Through His incarnation, we know Christ and God the Father in the experience of the covenant of His grace (Gen. 1:26–27).

---

15. Athanasius, *On the Incarnation*, 4:44.
16. Calvin, *Institutes*, 1.15.4.

> And as we have borne the image of the man of dust, we shall also bear the image of the heavenly Man. (1 Cor. 15:49)

> But we all, with unveiled face, beholding as in a mirror the glory of the Lord, are being transformed into the same image from glory to glory, just as by the Spirit of the Lord. (2 Cor. 3:18)

> Our gospel is veiled…to those…whose minds the god of this age has blinded, who do not believe, lest the light of the gospel of the glory of Christ, who is the image of God, should shine on them. (2 Cor. 4:3–4)

> Be renewed in the spirit of your mind…that you put on the new man which was created according to God, in true righteousness and holiness. (Eph. 4:23–24)

> You…have put on the new man who is renewed in knowledge according to the image of Him who created him. (Col. 3:9–10)

Athanasius described the purpose and result of the incarnation as the renewing in us of the image of God:

> What then was God to do? or what was to be done save the renewing of that which was in God's image, so that by it men might once more be able to know Him? But how could this have come to pass save by the presence of the very Image of God, our Lord Jesus Christ? For by men's means it was impossible, since they are but made after an image; nor by angels either, for not even they are (God's) images. Whence the Word of God came in His

own person, that, as He was the Image of the Father, He might be able to create afresh the man after the image.[17]

Since we were only *made in* God's image, we couldn't repair the damage we had done in the garden. Therefore, God sent His Son, who *is* the image of God, to begin repairing us from the inside out once again into the image of God. We desperately need a makeover of eternal proportions, and the incarnation of the Son dramatically accomplishes the change.

Destruction of Death

Another benefit of these mysterious doctrines of the incarnation and hypostatic union that Athanasius brought out in his classic work *On the Incarnation* was that the incarnation of the Word destroys death. This was necessary if the image of God within us was ever to be renewed. Athanasius stated it this way: "But, again, it could not else have taken place had not death and corruption been done away. Whence He took, in natural fitness, a mortal body, that while death might in it be once for all done away, men made after His Image might once more be renewed. None other then was sufficient for this need, save the Image of the Father."[18]

The Son of God put death on notice just by His incarnation. The One in whom was life (John 1:4) entered the realm of death and of him who had the power of death—that is, the devil (Heb. 2:14). He came on His terms, so to speak, and beat the devil at his game, dying because of our sins but rising

---

17. Athanasius, *On the Incarnation*, 4:43.
18. Athanasius, *On the Incarnation*, 4:43.

again in a new order of things to transform and renew all that He had made so good in the beginning.

Evangelism

In a multicultural society such as the United States, everyone's opinion about religion is assumed to be equally valid. The claim of the incarnation of the Son of God stands as a dividing line between biblical Christianity and all other religions—whether other forms of Christianity or world religious systems. The incarnation is a part of what the apostle Paul called the scandal of the gospel in 1 Corinthians 1:18–31. He explains that in their quest for wisdom, the Greeks saw spiritual things as being intrinsically good while earthly things were intrinsically evil. Because of this, the inevitable question was how an eternal and spiritual God could become a temporal and tangible man. This was a repulsive offense. It still is, as it excludes all those who don't believe its claim.

Yet the incarnation of the Lord holds out to the cultures of the world an inclusive gospel. The incarnation says that God's very own Son, His only Son, came from His heavenly dwelling place down to the sin-laden and sin-ravaged world and became a human being. This means that there is no one person or people group with whom the Lord didn't identify and become one in their humanity. This is why the Canons of Dort say, "Moreover, the promise of the gospel is that *whosoever* believes in Christ crucified shall not perish, but have eternal life. This promise, together with the command to repent and believe, ought to be declared and published *to all nations*, and to *all persons promiscuously and without distinction*, to whom God out of His good pleasure sends the gospel (II, 5).

Christian Comfort

Finally, Christ's incarnation and union of two natures in His one person speak of comfort. On the most basic and personal levels, knowing the Lord Christ as the God-man gives those who believe in His name the existential comfort of knowing that they have a Savior who is like them and who suffered like them in every way. There's no struggle the Christian will go through that the Savior does not understand. There's no tragedy that can befall a child of God that He doesn't know how to empathize and sympathize with.

Far from being abstract and meaningless, then, knowing what our Savior is like as God and as man, in two distinct natures united in one glorious person, is essential to know what Christianity's object is all about—Jesus Christ rescuing helpless sinners. It is essential to "grow in the grace and knowledge of our Lord and Savior Jesus Christ" (2 Peter 3:18).

Conclusion

In conclusion, we can summarize these mysteries about the Lord and Savior in no better way than to lay simply and poetically side by side the great truths of His divinity and humanity: the One who eternally was became something He eternally was not; the infinite became finite; the eternal became temporal; the immutable became mutable; the invisible became visible; the Creator became a creature; the Sustainer became dependent; the Almighty became weak; the divine became human; God became man.

> Thou who art God beyond all praising,
> All for love's sake becamest man;

Stooping so low, but sinners raising,
Heav'nward by thine eternal plan.
Thou who art God beyond all praising,
All for love's sake becamest man.[19]

---

19. Frank Houghton, "Thou Who Was Rich beyond All Splendor," in *Complete Mission Praise* (London: Marshall Pickering, 1999), #700.

SEVEN

The Christ of the Qur'an versus the Christ of the Bible

> When Jesus came into the region of Caesarea Philippi, He asked His disciples, saying, "Who do men say that I, the Son of Man, am?"
>
> —MATTHEW 16:13

As mentioned in the previous chapter, the Christian doctrine of the incarnation of the Son of God affects the church's calling in witness and evangelism. Because the Son of God came to earth and dwelt among humanity "to seek and to save that which was lost" (Luke 19:10), He commands us to "go" (Matt. 28:19) and empowers us with His Holy Spirit (Acts 1:8) to share this earth-shattering news with the world. In practice and proclamation, with life and lips, Jesus Christ enlists us who have been renewed into His image (Eph. 4:24; Col. 3:10) as the agents of this renewal in others. This means we need to be particularly sensitive to the philosophies, religions, and ideas around us so that we might be even more effective in this task. We need to be good listeners as Christians, "swift to hear, slow to speak" (James 1:19). We need to listen to the claims of our Muslim neighbors.[1]

Now that our vast world is increasingly a village, we're coming into contact with the claims of Islam like never before. As Christians, it's our duty to understand these claims and be prepared to counter them for the sake of the salvation of all those whom Christ will redeem "out of every tribe and tongue and people and nation" (Rev. 5:9). Living in our post-9/11 world with its reality of global terrorism, we must be aware not only of the politically motivated claims that Islam is a "religion of peace"[2] but that Muslims believe in Jesus Christ just as Christians do.[3]

The purpose of this book is to explain what the Holy Scriptures teach about the incarnation and two natures of the Son of God, our Lord Jesus Christ. It's important, therefore, to look at what the sacred book of Islam, the Qur'an, says about these themes and consider its claims. The man known as "the apostle to Islam," Samuel Zwemer (1867–1952), said,

---

[1]. For a brief introduction to Islam, see Alfred Guillaume, *Islam* (1956; repr., London: Penguin, 1990).

[2]. E.g., "Some of the comments that have been uttered about Islam do not reflect the sentiments of my government or the sentiments of most Americans. Islam, as practiced by the vast majority of people, is a peaceful religion, a religion that respects others. Ours is a country based upon tolerance and we welcome people of all faiths in America." George W. Bush, remarks to reporters, November 13, 2002, George W. Bush—The White House.gov, https://georgewbush-whitehouse.archives.gov/infocus/ramadan/islam.html.

[3]. E.g., the comment by Imam Fisal Hammouda, who in an interview with Bill Hybels at Willow Creek Community Church, said, "We believe in Jesus, more than you do in fact." As quoted in Sean D. Hamill, "Willow Creek Welcomes Muslim Cleric's Perspective," *Chicago Tribune*, October 12, 2001, https://www.chicagotribune.com/news/ct-xpm-2001-10-12-0110120236-story.html.

"There is no better way of preaching Christ to Muslims than by beginning with the testimony of the Koran to Jesus."[4]

Is the Christ of the Qur'an the same as the Christ of the Scriptures? Is the Christ of the Qur'an the same as the Christ of the ecumenical creeds? If the Muslim Christ isn't the same Christ whom Christians follow, then who is he? How do we Christians respond to the Islamic version of Jesus Christ? As Christians, we all are called to "test the spirits [that is, teachers], whether they are of God" (1 John 4:1). We must be willing and able to discern truth from error and then share the truth with those around us as Christ has called us.

The Christ of the Qur'an

Jesus Was Not and Is Not God

The most fundamental tenet of Islam is its declaration of faith called the *shahada*: "There is no god but God [Allah], and Muhammad is the messenger of God." Interestingly, this confession is nowhere to be found in the Qur'an. Nevertheless, what the Qur'an teaches about Jesus Christ starts from this premise. Of the explicit rejection of Jesus's divinity the Qur'an says, "The Jews call Uzair [Ezra] a son of Allah, and the Christians call Christ the Son of Allah. That is a saying from their mouth; (in this) they but imitate what the Unbelievers of old used to say. Allah's curse be on them: how they are deluded away from the Truth!" (9:30).[5]

---

4. Samuel M. Zwemer, "The Moslem Christ," in *Islam and the Cross: Selections from "The Apostle to Islam,"* ed. Roger S. Greenway (1912; repr., Phillipsburg, N.J.: P&R, 2002), 10.

5. All quotations from the Qur'an are from Presidency of Islamic Researches, *The Holy Qur-an: English Translation of the Meanings and*

A portion of 9:31 goes on to say, "And (they [Christians] take as their Lord) Christ the son of Mary; yet they were commanded to worship but One God." The commentary given on this *ayat* (verse) says, "Taking men for gods or sons of Allah was not a new thing. All ancient mythology have fables of that kind. There was less excuse for such blasphemies after the Prophets of Allah had clearly explained our true relation to Allah than in the times of primitive ignorance and superstition."

Therefore, because Jesus is not God, He is not omniscient like Allah. The text of Qur'an 5:116 states: "And behold! Allah will say: 'O Jesus the son of Mary! Didst thou say unto men, take me and my mother for two gods beside Allah?' He will say: 'Glory to Thee! Never could I say what I had no right (to say). Had I said such a thing Thou wouldst indeed have known it. Thou knowest what is in my heart, though I know not what is in Thine. For Thou knowest in full all that is hidden.'"

Furthermore, the Qur'an says of the prophet Muhammad: "Thus he taught men to worship and fear Allah, not himself: 'For Allah, He is my Lord and your Lord: so worship ye Him: this is a Straight Way'" (43:64). Jesus isn't divine in any way but is a mere man, according to the Qur'an. In the words of Islamic apologist Syed Ameer Ali (1849–1928), "That Jesus ever maintained he was the Son of God in the sense in which it has been construed by Christian divines and apologists we totally deny."[6]

Commentary (Al-Madinah Al-Munawarah, Saudi Arabia: Ministry of Hajj and endowments, 1993).

6. Syed Ameer Ali, *The Spirit of Islam: A History of the Evolution and Ideals of Islam* (1891; repr., New York: Cosimo Classics, 2010), 141.

Jesus Was Born of the Virgin Mary

What does the Qur'an say about the birth of Jesus? It may come as a surprise to Christians that the Qur'an teaches Jesus was born of a virgin. Sadly, we'll see below that this virgin birth is unlike the doctrine of the virgin birth in the Bible: "She said: 'O my Lord! How shall I have a son when no man hath touched me?' He said: 'Even so; Allah createth what He willeth: when He hath decreed a matter, He but saith to it, "Be," and it is!'" (3:47; cf. 19:21–22).

Although here is a clear affirmation of Jesus's virgin birth, the biblical teaching of the agent of this conception, the Holy Spirit, is omitted. According to the Qur'an, the virgin birth was an act of Allah's sheer will alone. This is typical of Allah when you read the Qur'an. He does things by brute sovereignty. This means that although Jesus was born of the virgin Mary, He's not called the "son of Allah," the son of God. This would be blasphemy according to the Qur'an because it would affirm His deity. Instead, Jesus is simply called "the son of Mary" repeatedly (cf. 3:45; 4:157; 5:17, 75, 110, 112, 116; 9:31; 19:34; 23:50; 43:6; 61:6).

Jesus Was Sinless

As an aside, while the Qur'an doesn't say Jesus was sinless, Islamic tradition (hadith) does. One tradition says, "Abu Huraira reported God's messenger [Muhammad] as saying, 'Except Mary and her son, no human being is born without the devil touching him, so that he raises his voice crying out because of the devil's touch.'"[7] Zwemer recounts the com-

---

7. Mishkat al-Masabih, https://sunnah.com/mishkat/1.

mentator Er-Razi as saying Jesus was given the title Messiah "because he was kept clear from the taint of sin."[8]

Finally, in the tradition called Sahih al-Bukhari, considered by the vast majority of Muslim scholars as the most authentic reports of Muhammad's sayings, there is this fascinating discussion. Muhammad is reported to have said that "Allah will gather the believers on the Day of Resurrection in the same way (as they are gathered in this life), and they will say, 'Let us ask someone to intercede for us with our Lord that He may relieve us from this place of ours.'" It's interesting to note what this implies: *believers* are suffering at the hands of Allah and need intercession so that Allah will change their experience. This implication is then explicit at the end when Muhammad intercedes, leaves Allah's presence, and goes into hellfire to bring out all who confess "there is no god but Allah" and who "has in his heart good equal to the weight of a barley grain, a wheat grain, or an atom (or a smallest ant)." Back to the beginning, though, believers first will go to Adam: "O Adam! Don't you see the people (people's condition)? Allah created you with His Own Hands and ordered His angels to prostrate before you, and taught you the names of all the things. Please intercede for us with our Lord so that He may relieve us from this place of ours."

But Adam will say, "I am not fit for this undertaking," mention his sins, and then refer them to Noah. When the believers go to Noah, Noah will say the same: "I am not fit for this undertaking," mention his sins, and then refer them to Abraham. The believers receive the same responses from

---

8. Zwemer, "Moslem Christ," 12.

both Abraham and then Moses. But Moses sends them to Jesus, "Allah's slave and His Apostle and His Word (Be: And it was) and a soul created by Him." Jesus will say to believers, "I am not fit for this undertaking, but you'd better go to Muhammad whose sins of the past and the future had been forgiven (by Allah)." Notice that Jesus doesn't mention His own "mistakes" but says that Muhammad was a sinner and needed forgiveness from Allah! According to the most trusted Muslim source, Muhammad confessed himself to be a sinner and Jesus sinless.[9]

Jesus Was Merely Human
Since Jesus isn't proclaimed as the Son of God, the Christ of the Qur'an is simply a human, albeit sinless. Islam teaches that Jesus wasn't, isn't, and never will be God. This is seen in all the references concerning His title "the son of Mary." As Christians, we too affirm that Jesus was the son of Mary, but this is where the Qur'an stops and affirms nothing more about His being and nature: "Christ the son of Mary was no more than a Messenger; many were the Messengers that passed away before him. His mother was a woman of truth. They had both to eat their (daily) food. See how Allah doth make His Signs clear to them; yet see in what ways they are deluded away from the truth" (5:75).

The fact that Jesus had to eat just like Mary was a sign from Allah that Jesus was nothing more than any other human being. According to Islamic belief, those who affirm Christ's deity are "deluded." He was just a highly favored

---

9. Sahih al-Bukhari, https://sunnah.com/bukhari/97.

servant: "He was no more than a servant: we granted our favour to him, and we made him an example to the Children of Israel" (43:59). He was created as a man just like Adam by Allah: "The similitude of Jesus before Allah is as that of Adam; He created him from the dust, then said to him: 'Be': and he was" (3:59). As Adam was a man, so was Jesus Christ. If He looked like a man, ate like a man, and had a mother like a man, the Qur'an concludes, He was a man.

Jesus Was a Righteous Prophet

Furthermore, according to 6:85, Jesus is ranked with Zakariya (Zachariah) and his son, John (the Baptist), and Elias (Elijah) as righteous prophets. This is also the testimony of 3:45–46: "Behold! the angels said: 'O Mary! Allah giveth thee glad tidings of a Word from Him: his name will be called Christ Jesus, the son of Mary, held in honour in this world and the Hereafter and of (the company of) those nearest to Allah; He shall speak to the people in childhood and maturity. And He shall be (of the company) of the righteous.'"

Christ's prophetic purpose was to confirm the Torah (Taurat) and to bring the gospel (Injil), according to 5:46. As 61:6 says, "And remember, Jesus, the son of Mary, said: 'O Children of Israel! I am the messenger of Allah (sent) to you, confirming the Taurat [Torah] (which came) before me, and giving Glad Tidings of a messenger to come after me, whose name shall be Ahmad.'"

Jesus affirmed His own prophethood while still in the cradle, according to 19:30, saying, "I am indeed a servant of Allah: He hath given me revelation and made me a prophet." He is also described as an eschatological prophet in 43:61, where we read: "And (Jesus) shall be a Sign (for the coming of) the Hour (of Judgment); therefore have no doubt about the (Hour), but follow ye Me: this is a Straight Way."

Jesus Performed Miracles
As a sinless and righteous prophet, Jesus Christ performed many miracles, as did the prophets of old. In 3:48–51 of the Qur'an we read of His miracles:

> [From above]…I have come to you, with a sign from your Lord, in that I make for you out of clay, as it were, the figure of a bird, and breathe into it, and it becomes a bird by Allah's leave: And I heal those born blind, and the lepers, and I bring the dead into life by Allah's leave; and I declare to you what ye eat, and what ye store in your houses. Surely therein is a sign for you if ye did believe; (I have come to you), to attest the Torah which was before me. And to make lawful to you part of what was (before) forbidden to you; I have come to you with a sign from your Lord. So fear Allah, and obey me. It is Allah who is my Lord and your Lord; then worship Him. This is a Way that is straight.

Jesus Was Not Crucified
The last point the Qur'an makes about Jesus Christ is that He wasn't crucified. Instead, the commentary on 3:46 seeks to clarify what really happened. At the age of thirty-three, Jesus "in the eyes of his enemies…was crucified."[10] While the enemies of Jesus thought they saw Him on the cross, 3:55 speaks

---

10. Qur'an, 154n388.

of what did happen to Jesus in being caught up to Allah: "Behold! Allah said: 'O Jesus! I will take thee and raise thee to Myself and clear thee (of the falsehoods) of those who blaspheme; I will make those who follow thee superior to those who reject faith, to the Day of Resurrection: then shall ye all return unto me, and I will judge between you of the matters wherein ye dispute.'"

Later in the Qur'an, this teaching is reiterated: "They said (in boast), 'We have killed Christ Jesus the son of Mary, the Messenger of Allah'; but they killed him not, nor crucified him. Only a likeness of that was shown to them. And those who differ therein are full of doubts, with no (certain) knowledge. But only conjecture to follow, for of a surety they killed him not;—nay, Allah raised him up unto Himself; and Allah is Exalted in Power, Wise" (4:157–58).

The commentary on this portion of the Qur'an, again, is telling as to the beliefs of Islam. It says, "Jesus was charged by the Jews with blasphemy as claiming to be Allah or the son of Allah. The Christians adopted the substance of the claim and made it the cornerstone of their faith. Allah clears Jesus of such a charge or claim."[11] In contrast to the Christians, "they [true believers] disbelieved indeed those that say that Allah is Christ the son of Mary. Say: 'Who then hath the least power against Allah, if His Will were to destroy Christ, the son of Mary, his mother, and all—every one that is on the earth? For to Allah belongeth the dominion of the heavens and the earth, and all that is between. He createth what He pleaseth. For Allah hath power over all things" (5:17).

---

11. Qur'an, 157n395.

According to Islam, then, Jesus was not crucified. While His enemies thought He was, He really was taken up into heaven. Without a crucifixion, there's no resurrection. Without a resurrection, Jesus is not a Savior as God-in-flesh.

An Evangelistic Bridge or Chasm?

Based on the claims of the Qur'an, the Islamic teachings concerning Jesus Christ are against the New Testament as confessed in the historic Christian creeds. Muslims believe Christians are idolaters; Christians believe the claims of Islam are false. In the language of the New Testament, as we "test the spirit" of the Qur'an we find it to be antichrist. The apostle John used this denunciation of those who do "not confess that Jesus Christ has come in the flesh" (1 John 4:3; cf. 2 John 7).

So we're at an impasse. The Islamic beliefs about Jesus are an evangelistic bridge that gets us only partway across this chasm. Both groups affirm Jesus's virgin birth, sinless life, miracles, and prophetic preaching. But this is not enough of a bridge. As Zwemer said, "Mohammed leads his followers to the portal, but he fails to open the door."[12] The Christology of the Qur'an is an obstacle in evangelism and apologetics to our Muslim neighbors. Although they may use terminology similar to ours, we must note the different definitions they assume. When they speak of Jesus Christ, they have a completely different definition and person in mind from Christians. There's still an enormous chasm to cross as we seek to communicate the good news of Jesus to Muslims. As Zwemer said, "Islam denies the need of Christ as Mediator,

---

12. Zwemer, "Moslem Christ," 3.

only to substitute Mohammed as a mediator, without an incarnation, without an atonement, and without a demand for a change of character."[13]

To switch metaphors, the Christology of the Qur'an is a building block of common ground between Christians and Muslims insofar as we recognize some similarity but vast differences. In many ways, the Qur'an is a stumbling stone for Muslims; their holy book dims the light of truth found in the Bible. This common ground gets us only so far in our witness with Muslims. They are still in need of regeneration from spiritual death to life and enlightenment by the Holy Spirit to acknowledge their sins against God and understand that the truth of the gospel is the remedy. Christians say of Muslims what Muslims say of Christians: they're nonbelievers. Muslims affirm something of the Jesus of history and Scripture but are still dead in their sins and are blinded by the "god of this age" (2 Cor. 4:4; see chapters 3–4). We must keep all these things in mind when we speak with our Muslim neighbors. The Qur'an is insufficient for salvation; the hope the gospel of Jesus Christ brings to all sinners as found in the Scriptures alone must be opened up.

The Christ of the Bible

Our Muslim neighbors speak of Jesus, and so do we, but our definitions of similar words differ. The challenge is to listen intently. One Islamic poet expressed his questions like this:

> You who worship Jesus, I have a question for you,
>   and can you answer it?

---

13. Zwemer, "Moslem Christ," 24.

The Christ of the Qur'an versus the Christ of the Bible 147

If Jesus was Almighty God, with power to strike terror
into all men,
Why do you believe that the Jews could make him
endure the agony of the Cross?
And why do you believe that God died, and was
buried in the dust,
And sought from his creatures a draught of water,
that he might quench his fiery thirst?…

And that he died a miserable death in an agony of thirst?
And that they put on his head a crown of thorns….

And that the blood flowed down his cheeks, and
stained his face like henna?
And that he rode on a donkey's colt to save himself
from the toil of the journey?…

And if he was God as you suppose, why did he pray
to be delivered from the torment?
And who restored his Spirit when it left his body?
And who kept the world in its state until he came
back from the dead?
Was there a second Lord watching its affairs?
Or did he suffer it to go to destruction?
And was he crucified for some evil he had done?
Or why did he merit the punishment?…

And was he himself pleased with the crucifixion, or
angry? Tell me truly.
And if you say he was pleased with it in order that he
might atone for the fault of the repentant,
I say that Adam sinned and repented by the grace of
God, and God forgave him….
And if you say that the cross was forced on him in
spite of himself:

> Then this Almighty God is not Almighty, for he hung
>   on the Cross, cursed on every side as it is written.
> Do not blame me for thus putting the matter.
> Answer my questions.
> And do not fail, because silence in this is a
>   disgrace to you.
> I have given you advice, and desire only that it may
>   profit you.
> For myself, I will die a firm believer in the religion
> of Mohammed, the noblest of men.
> As I do not wish to see the horrors of the day of
>   judgment.[14]

Let's take up the challenge of giving answers to questions like these. We'll focus on one short passage, Hebrews 1:1–3, which offers a concise summary of the person and work of our Lord Jesus Christ. The purpose of this passage is to demonstrate that Jesus is better and greater than all the old covenant prophets because He's the one they looked forward to.

The Final Word

Hebrews begins by using two synonyms together, "various times" and "various ways" (*polumerōs kai polutropōs*; Heb. 1:1), in order to emphasize one main point: the revelation of the old covenant was more than abundant. The question in the writer's mind is not the variety of modes of revelation (vision, dream, prophecy) or the different times in which they took place (Abraham, Moses, Isaiah) but whether God's revelation is complete. The author says that the former revelation

---

14. As quoted in Zwemer, "Moslem Christ," 7, 8, 9.

through prophets, though adequate, was partial or piecemeal. In contrast, now in the revelation of the Son from heaven, God has spoken definitively and finally. This text alone disproves the presupposition of Islam: that God still needed to speak a final word to the world through another prophet. God's Word is here in the revelation of the Son, in fulfillment of the prophets and explained by the apostles who witnessed His life and resurrection.[15]

The author of Hebrews makes this point with an explicit contrast between God's speech "in time past" and "in these last days" (1:1–2). In the Septuagint, the Greek translation of the Old Testament, the phrase "last days/latter days" is used in the translation of many texts (e.g., Gen. 49:1; Num. 24:14; Isa. 2:2; Jer. 23:20; Ezek. 38:16; Dan. 10:14; Hos. 3:5; Mic. 4:1). But the author of Hebrews adds the little word "these" (v. 2) to this phrase. He is emphasizing that the days in which his audience was then (and now) living are the last days, the age of fulfillment spoken of by the prophets.

F. F. Bruce summarized the meaning of Hebrews 1:1–3: "The story of divine revelation is a story of progression up to Christ, but there is no progression beyond Him."[16] Therefore, a direct word of God is spoken to us that "there is no further reason why we should be in doubt whether to expect any new revelation. It was not a part of the Word that Christ brought,

---

15. See Samuel M. Zwemer, "Christianity as Final Religion," in *Christianity the Final Religion: Addresses on the Missionary Message for the World Today, Showing That the Old Gospel Is the Only Gospel* (Grand Rapids: Eerdmans-Sevensma, 1920), 95–109.

16. F. F. Bruce, *The Epistle to the Hebrews*, New International Commentary on the New Testament (Grand Rapids: Eerdmans, 1964), 3.

but the last closing Word."[17] So unlike the Qur'an, which says that Jesus was a great prophet who only pronounced the day of Muhammad (the "other Comforter"), Hebrews 1:1–3 proclaims that Christ is *the* final revelation of God. In Christ, all God's revelation is summarized. There is nothing more and no one else to come.

So who is this Son in whom God has spoken? What makes Him different from the Christ of the Qur'an? In Hebrews 1:2–3 the author gives us the Son's credentials, pedigree, distinct titles, and activities. As if being the climactic Word of God isn't enough, seven more descriptions of His work follow: "heir of all things," "through whom also [God] made the worlds" (v. 2), "the brightness of [God's] glory," "the express image of [God's] person," the upholder of "all things by the word of His power," the One who "purged our sins," and finally who "sat down at the right hand of the Majesty on high" (v. 3). The apostolic words, therefore, gloriously answer the questions of our Muslim neighbors. In these words, we clearly see who Jesus Christ is in contrast to the Qur'an of Islam.

Heir of All Things

Hebrews proclaims that the Son is the final Word from God because He is "heir of all things" (1:2). This means that He rightfully inherits whatever the Father has stipulated in His will for Him. He, not Muhammad, is the most esteemed and highly honored of the Father. He's the Son of the Father,

---

17. John Calvin, *The Epistle of Paul the Apostle to the Hebrews and the First and Second Epistles of St. Peter*, trans. William B. Johnston, vol. 12 of *Calvin's Commentaries*, ed. David W. Torrance and Thomas F. Torrance (Grand Rapids: Eerdmans, 1963), 6.

unlike the portrait of Christ in the Qur'an, in which He is merely the son of Mary.

So when did the Father "appoint" Jesus Christ the heir of all things? This happened at His glorious resurrection after He was crucified for our sins, unlike in Islam. Hebrews uses the language of Psalm 2:8:

> Ask of Me, and I will give You
> The nations for Your inheritance,
> And the ends of the earth for Your possession.

This is the only place in Hebrews where Christ is called "heir." The other two uses of "heir(s)" are in reference to believers (6:17) and Noah (11:7). As John Calvin said, "The name 'heir' is attributed to Christ as manifested in the flesh; for in being made man and putting on the same nature as us, He took on Himself this heirship, in order to restore to us what we had lost in Adam."[18]

So what is the content of His inheritance? The innumerable company of the redeemed and the universe renewed by virtue of His triumphant work of reconciliation. The promise of inheritance in Psalm 2:8 is universalized—that is, its scope is enlarged to the infinite power. For He's not only the heir of the peoples of the earth and their lands; He's the heir of "all things." Christ will inherit all things in their glorious renewal when He returns at the end of the age.

---

18. Calvin, *Epistle…to the Hebrews*, 7.

Through Whom Also God Made the Worlds

As the glorified Son, Jesus isn't only the heir of all things but also their Creator. This means He's unmistakably God. Through Him God the Father made the "worlds" (*aiōnas*)—that is, all periods of time and everything contained in them. This is the testimony of the New Testament: God, who made "the heavens and the earth" in the beginning is our Lord Jesus Christ—the eternal Word (e.g., John 1:1–3). In Colossians 1:16 we see that Christ made "all things." These things are defined as everything in heaven and earth, visible and invisible, thrones and dominions, principalities and powers. John says in the beautiful prologue to his gospel: "All things were made through Him" (John 1:3). Paul says at the end of his magnificent hymn, "For of Him and through Him and to Him are all things, to whom be glory forever. Amen" (Rom. 11:36). In 1 Corinthians 8:6 the apostle says there is one Father and one Lord Jesus Christ "through whom are all things." Therefore Jesus is greater than the prophets, including Muhammad, who claims to be a prophet. Jesus didn't just create the prophets but He created the time and space in which they spoke to the fathers in times past.

The Brightness of the Father's Glory

Our Lord Jesus Christ is greater than Muhammad because He's the "brightness"—that is, the effulgence, the splendor—of the Father's glory. All that the Father is, the Son reflects. The Father's glory is the Son's glory: "The Word became flesh and dwelt among us, and we beheld His glory" (John 1:14). The glory of the bush that was on fire but didn't burn (Exodus 3), the glory of Mount Sinai (Exodus 20) that was so overwhelming Moses had to put a veil over his face (Exodus 34), and the shekinah glory of the tabernacle (Exodus 40) and temple (1 Kings 8) became human in Jesus.

The Express Image of the Father's Person

As the final revelation of God, the Son is greater than the prophets. Another reason is because He is the exact image of the essence of the Father. According to the Nicene Creed, He is "God of God, Light of Light, very God of very God." Jesus Christ is the image of God par excellence (2 Cor. 4:4; Col. 1:15). He is the second Adam (Rom. 5:14; 1 Cor. 15:45–49); in Him all that was lost by sin is regained. But Christ is not just second Adam as to His human nature, as in Islam; He is the second person of the Trinity as to His divine nature from all eternity.

Upholding All Things by the Word of His Power

The Christ of the Scriptures not only made all things but continues to be the providential upholder of "all things" (Heb. 1:3). He upholds not only the material universe but also the times and seasons. How does He do this? He accomplishes this by means of "the word of His power." The word God spoke at creation, "Let there be," finds its result, "it was so," in Christ. Paul described this powerful work of the Son, saying, "In Him all things consist" (Col. 1:17). This means that every atom; every molecule; every person, place, and thing are held together by the Son. Without His providential upholding, everything would fall apart into chaos and oblivion.

He Purged Our Sins

The Creator and Sustainer in the person of the Son became incarnate and died for the sins of His people. He made "atonement" for our sins as in the Old Testament sacrificial system (Lev. 16:4–5, 29–34). Clearly the Bible and the Qur'an are antithetical in this. When people say that Christianity and Islam are mutual and compatible, they're deceived. Islam says, "You do the work"; Christianity says, "Christ did the work." Islam says that you're saved by your obedience to the law; Christianity says that you're saved by Christ's obedience to the law. Islam says that Christ didn't die; Christianity says that Christ died for our sins—and without Christ's sacrifice, there's no salvation, no forgiveness, and no fellowship with God: "without shedding of blood there is no remission" (Heb. 9:22).

Sat Down on the Right Hand of the Majesty on High

Finally, the Son incarnate is the ascended and exalted Son at the right hand of God. The idea of sitting down (Rom. 8:34; Eph. 1:20; Col. 3:1; Heb. 1:13; 8:1; 10:12; 12:2) means that He has provided perfect sacrifice. He has completed His mission and is now honored at the right hand of the heavenly King. There He intercedes for us (Heb. 7:25) to preserve us in this present evil age.

Conclusion

The Jesus Christ of the Islamic faith as found in the Qur'an is not the Jesus Christ of the Bible. In Islam Jesus isn't considered to be God; He isn't considered to be the Savior. Therefore, the biblical conclusion about Islam is that our Muslim neighbors are still in their sins. The Holy Scriptures proclaim Jesus not only the prophet par excellence but also the eternal God made incarnate "for us and for our salvation." We must strive not only to present to our Muslim neighbors the theological errors of Islam but also the true gospel of Christ with respect and gentleness (1 Peter 3:15). This goes against our politically correct sensibilities, but as Zwemer said, "The only Christianity that has a missionary message for the Muslim world is this vital Christianity."[19] As stated in the previous chapter, the incarnation of the Son of God as our Lord Jesus Christ holds out to all cultures and religions of the world an inclusive gospel in which the Savior says to all, "Come to Me, all you who labor and are heavy laden, and I will give you rest" (Matt. 11:28).

We must be ready to explain the hope that we have within us to a world that seeks answers to their inward longing. God dwelt among us, and we beheld His glory. Yes, the One who existed from the beginning is Jesus Christ, the Word of life. Therefore, we must testify and announce the hope of eternal life offered in Christ alone. Let us diligently share the good news of the person and work of Jesus Christ with all those we encounter for the glory of the One who came to seek and to save humanity from the wages of sin.

> Jesus, my Shepherd, Brother, Friend,
> My Prophet, Priest, and King,
> My Lord, my Life, my Way, my End,
> Accept the praise I bring.[20]

---

19. Zwemer, "Moslem Christ," 27.
20. John Newton, "How Sweet the Name of Jesus Sounds," in *Trinity Psalter Hymnal*, #492.

APPENDIX 1

The Ecumenical Creeds

The Apostles' Creed
The Apostles' Creed was not actually written by the apostles themselves but rather was developed over the course of time by the ancient churches (AD 100–700). The earliest versions of what would later become the Apostles' Creed were used in Rome in the second century as a way to instruct converts who were preparing for baptism (cf. Eph. 4:4–6). It's been called the Apostles' Creed because it is founded on the apostolic authority of the apostles' doctrine in the Scriptures.

The Apostles' Creed confesses succinctly what the baptized Christian believes: there is one God who exists in three persons. This is called the doctrine of the Holy Trinity. In confessing this about God, the Creed is outlined in three parts, following the order of each person of the Trinity. In the first part, we confess to believe in God the Father, our Creator; in the second part, we confess to believe in Jesus Christ, our Redeemer; and in the third part, we confess to believe in the Holy Spirit, our Sanctifier (cf. Heidelberg Catechism 24).[1]

---

1. Adapted from Hyde, *Good Confession*, 19. The most comprehensive and scholarly study of the history of the Apostles' Creed in English is Liuwe H. Westra, *The Apostles' Creed: Origin, History, and Some Early Commentaries*,

I believe in GOD THE FATHER Almighty; Maker of heaven and earth.

And in JESUS CHRIST, His only (begotten) Son our Lord; who was conceived by the Holy Ghost, born of the Virgin Mary; suffered under Pontius Pilate, was crucified, dead, and buried; he descended into hell; the third day he rose from the dead; he ascended into heaven, and sitteth at the right hand of God the Father Almighty; from thence he shall come to judge the quick and the dead.

I believe in the HOLY GHOST; the holy catholic Church; the communion of saints; the forgiveness of sins; the resurrection of the body; and the life everlasting. Amen.[2]

The Nicene Creed

The Nicene Creed was written in AD 325 at the first ecumenical Council of Nicea, a city in modern-day Turkey. Representatives from throughout the church gathered to respond to and to reject the false teaching of a preacher named Arius. Arius taught that the Son of God was not eternal but was the first creation of God the Father. This meant that Jesus Christ was less divine than God the Father. Later, at the second ecumenical Council of Constantinople in 381, the churches responded to the false teaching of the Macedonians, who said that the Holy Spirit was not fully God. Thus, the

---

Instrumenta Patristica et Mediaevalia 43 (Turnhout, Belgium: Brepolis, 2002). For a survey of this history as it relates to the "descent into hell" clause in the Creed, see Daniel R. Hyde, *In Defense of the Descent: A Response to Contemporary Critics* (Grand Rapids: Reformation Heritage Books, 2010).

2. Schaff, *Creeds*, 2:45.

phrases about the Holy Spirit in the great Nicene Creed were added to complete it. Therefore, it is often called the Nicaeno-Constantinopolitan Creed. Because of its deep confession of the orthodox faith of the early Christian church and its purpose of protecting it, the Nicene Creed is the most important of the ancient Christian creeds. It was confessed by both the Greek-speaking and the Latin-speaking churches, although with one important difference. The Latin-speaking Western church insisted on the inclusion of the phrase "and the Son" (known as the *filioque*) in the article on the procession of the Holy Spirit, which was repudiated by the Eastern church from the time it was included in the West. In the Nicene Creed, we confess to believe in God the Father, God the Son, and God the Holy Spirit, as well as confess the church of Christ.[3]

> I believe in one GOD THE FATHER Almighty; Maker of heaven and earth, and of all things visible and invisible.
>
> And in one Lord JESUS CHRIST, the only-begotten Son of God, begotten of the Father before all worlds [God of God], Light of Light, very God of very God; begotten, not made, being of one substance [essence] with the Father; by whom all things were made. Who, for us men and for our salvation, came down from heaven, and was incarnate by the Holy Ghost of the Virgin Mary, and was made man; and was crucified also for us under Pontius Pilate; he suffered and was buried; and

---

3. Adapted from Hyde, *Good Confession*, 20. For a recent study guide through the Nicene Creed, see L. Charles Jackson, *Faith of Our Fathers: A Study of the Nicene Creed* (Moscow, Idaho: Canon Press, 2007).

the third day he rose again, according to the Scriptures; and ascended into heaven, and sitteth on the right hand of the Father; and he shall come again, with glory, to judge both the quick and the dead; whose kingdom shall have no end.

And [I believe] in the Holy Ghost, the Lord and Giver of Life; who proceedeth from the Father [and the Son]; who with the Father and the Son together is worshipped and glorified; who spake by the Prophets. And [I believe] one Holy Catholic and Apostolic Church. I acknowledge one Baptism for the remission of sins; and I look for the resurrection of the dead, and the life of the world to come. Amen.[4]

The Athanasian Creed

The Athanasian Creed, also known as *Quicunque Vult*, after the opening phrase in the Latin original, is named after Athanasius, who was a deacon in the church in Alexandria, Egypt. Athanasius was one of the staunchest opponents of the teachings of Arius against the doctrine of the Trinity at the Council of Nicea. Like the Apostles' Creed, the Athanasian Creed was most likely not written by its namesake but was taken from his writings against Arius and translated into Latin. These different parts of his writings were later compiled into a beautifully poetic creed sometime between AD 500 and 800. The creed is recognized in the Western churches but not by the Eastern, Greek-speaking churches.

---

4. Schaff, *Creeds*, 2:58–59.

The Athanasian Creed is more theologically advanced than the Apostles' and the Nicene Creeds and is divided into two parts. The first part confesses the doctrine of the Trinity: that we believe and worship one God in unity and unity in Trinity (§§3–28). The second part confesses the doctrine of the person of Christ: that there is one Lord Jesus Christ, who is both perfect God and perfect man (§§29–43). Both of these parts of the creed open with a statement of the necessity to believe in the triune nature of God and the two natures of Christ for salvation (§§1, 44).[5]

---

1. Whosoever will be saved, before all things it is necessary that he hold the catholic Faith:

2. Which faith except every one do keep whole and undefiled: without doubt he shall perish everlastingly.

3. And the catholic Faith is this: That we worship one God in Trinity, and Trinity in Unity;

4. Neither confounding the Persons: nor dividing the substance [essence].

5. For there is one Person of the Father: another of the Son: and another of the Holy Ghost.

6. But the Godhead of the Father, of the Son, and of the Holy Ghost, is all one: the glory equal, the majesty coeternal.

7. Such as the Father is: such is the Son: and such is the Holy Ghost.

---

5. Adapted from Hyde, *Good Confession*, 20.

8. The Father uncreate, [uncreated]: the Son uncreate, [uncreated]: and the Holy Ghost uncreate [uncreated].

9. The Father incomprehensible, [unlimited]: the Son incomprehensible, [unlimited]: and the Holy Ghost incomprehensible [unlimited, or infinite].

10. The Father eternal, the Son eternal, and the Holy Ghost eternal.

11. And yet they are not three eternals, but one eternal.

12. As also there are not three uncreated: nor three incomprehensibles [infinites], but one uncreated and one incomprehensible [infinite].

13. So likewise the Father is almighty, the Son almighty, and the Holy Ghost almighty.

14. And yet they are not three almighties, but one almighty.

15. So the Father is God, the Son is God, and the Holy Ghost is God;

16. And yet they are not three Gods: but one God.

17. So likewise the Father is Lord, the Son Lord, and the Holy Ghost Lord.

18. And yet not three Lords, but one Lord.

19. For like as we are compelled by the Christian verity to acknowledge every Person by himself to be God and Lord;

20. So are we forbidden by the catholic religion to say: There are three Gods, or three Lords.

21. The Father is made of none, neither created, nor begotten.

22. The Son is of the Father alone; neither made, nor created, but begotten.

23. The Holy Ghost is of the Father and of the Son; neither made, nor created, nor begotten, but proceeding.

24. So there is one Father, not three Fathers; one Son, not three Sons: one Holy Ghost, not three Holy Ghosts.

25. And in this Trinity none is afore, or after another, none is greater, or less than another [there is nothing before or after; nothing greater or less].

26. But the whole three Persons are coeternal, and coequal.

27. So that in all things, as aforesaid: the Unity in Trinity, and the Trinity in Unity, is to be worshipped.

28. He therefore that will be saved must thus think of the Trinity.

29. Furthermore it is necessary to everlasting salvation that he also believe rightly [faithfully] the incarnation of our Lord Jesus Christ.

30. For the right faith is that we believe and confess: that our Lord Jesus Christ, the Son of God, is God and man.

31. God, of the substance [essence] of the Father; begotten before the worlds: and made of the substance [essence] of his mother, born in the world.

32. Perfect God and perfect man, of a reasonable soul and human flesh subsisting.

33. Equal to the Father, as touching his Godhead, and inferior to the Father as touching his manhood.

34. Who although He is God and man, yet he is not two, but one Christ.

35. One, not by conversion of the Godhead into flesh, but by taking [assumption] of the manhood into God.

36. One altogether, not by confusion of substance, but by unity of Person.

37. For as the reasonable soul and flesh is one man, so God and man is one Christ;

38. Who suffered for our salvation, descended into hell, rose again the third day from the dead.

39. He ascended into heaven, he sitteth on the right hand of the Father God Almighty;

40. From whence [thence] he shall come to judge the quick and the dead.

41. At whose coming all men shall rise again with their bodies;

42. And shall give account for their own works.

43. And they that have done good shall go into life everlasting: and they that have done evil, into everlasting fire.

44. This is the Catholic Faith: which except a man believe faithfully [truly and firmly], he can not be saved.[6]

The Definition of Chalcedon

The Definition of Chalcedon was written in AD 451 at the fourth ecumenical Council of Chalcedon, a modern-day city

---

6. Schaff, *Creeds*, 2:66–70.

in Turkey. At this council, the churches of the ancient world gathered to respond to several different false teachings about who our Lord Jesus Christ is.

The Council asked, "In what sense was Jesus truly man?" and, "How was He both God and man?" Many answers had been given: Nestorianism taught that Christ's two natures—His divinity and humanity—were divided so that Christ was two completely separate persons and not united in the one person of Christ. Eutychianism taught that Christ's natures were so united in His person that the divine nature swallowed up the human nature, thus leaving one mixed nature. Apollinarianism taught that Jesus had a true human body and a "lower soul" (which animals have), but that the eternal logos (the "Word" of John 1:1) replaced the "higher soul" (which only humans have). This meant that Jesus Christ was not fully human like the rest of humanity. In one paragraph, the ancient theologians, pastors, and church leaders responded to these false teachings and confessed what Scripture taught on the vital doctrine of Christ: He is *one* Lord Jesus Christ in which are two natures—a divine and a human. In the Belgic Confession of Faith, article 9, the Reformed churches confess that "we do willingly receive the three creeds, namely, that of the Apostles, of Nicea, and of Athanasius; likewise that which, conformable thereunto, is agreed upon by the ancient fathers." The Definition of Chalcedon explains who the Jesus Christ of the three great ecumenical creeds is.[7]

---

7. Adapted from Hyde, *Good Confession*, 20–21. On Belgic Confession, art. 9, see Hyde, *With Heart and Mouth*, 123–35.

We, then, following the holy Fathers, all with one consent, teach men to confess one and the same Son, our Lord Jesus Christ, the same perfect in Godhead and also perfect in manhood; truly God and truly man, of a reasonable [rational] soul and body; consubstantial [coessential] with the Father according to the Godhead, and consubstantial with us according to the Manhood; in all things like unto us, without sin; begotten before all ages of the Father according to the Godhead, and in these latter days, for us and for our salvation, born of the Virgin Mary, the Mother of God, according to the Manhood; one and the same Christ, Son, Lord, Only-begotten, to be acknowledged in two natures, *inconfusedly, unchangeably, indivisibly, inseparably*; the distinction of natures being by no means taken away by the union, but rather the property of each nature being preserved, and concurring in one Person and one Subsistence, not parted or divided into two persons, but one and the same Son, and only begotten, God the Word, the Lord Jesus Christ, as the prophets from the beginning [have declared] concerning him, and the Lord Jesus Christ himself has taught us, and the Creed of the holy Fathers has handed down to us.[8]

---

8. Schaff, *Creeds*, 2:62–63.

APPENDIX 2

The Seven Ecumenical Councils

City	Year	Decision
Nicea	325	Rejected Arianism (the Son of God was the first creation of God the Father) and affirmed that the Son of God is of the same essence (*homoousion*) as the Father. Wrote the Nicene Creed.
Constantinople	381	Rejected the teachings of the Macedonians, who denied the deity of the Holy Spirit. Expanded the Nicene Creed.
Ephesus	431	Christ was affirmed to be one person with two full and complete natures against the views of Apollinarius (the "rational soul" of Jesus was replaced by the Logos) and Nestorius (who separated the two natures so that He was two persons).

Chalcedon	451	Rejected the teachings of the Eutyches, who said the humanity of Jesus was absorbed by the deity of the Son, and wrote the Definition of Chalcedon, which declared that Jesus is consubstantial with His Father according to His divine nature and consubstantial with people according to His human nature, and that these two natures are not confused, changed, divided, or separated.
Constantinople	553	Affirmed the first four councils, especially Chalcedon, which was being attacked by heretics.
Constantinople	680–681	Condemned Monothelism (which said Christ has only one will) and affirmed that Christ has two wills, a divine and a human will, which work in harmony.
Nicea	787	Declared that the reverencing of icons of Christ and the saints was legitimate.[1]

---

1. Reformed churches reject the declaration of this council as a violation of the second commandment (e.g., Heidelberg Catechism 96; Westminster Larger Catechism 109). For more on the subject of images of Jesus Christ, see Daniel R. Hyde, *In Living Color: Images of Christ and the Means of Grace* (Grandville, Mich.: Reformed Fellowship, 2008).

APPENDIX 3

The Tome of Leo I

At the center of the controversy with Eutyches in the mid-fifth century was a letter from Leo I, bishop of Rome, to Flavian, bishop of Constantinople, expressing the orthodox Christian understanding of the person and natures of the Lord Jesus Christ. What follows is the heart of that letter, which became influential at the Council of Chalcedon in 451.

> II. …The whole body of the faithful confess that they *believe in God the Father Almighty, and in Jesus Christ, His only Son, our Lord, who was born of the Holy Spirit and the Virgin Mary*. By which three statements the devices of almost all heretics are overthrown. For not only is God believed to be both Almighty and the Father, but the Son is shown to be co-eternal with Him, differing in nothing from the Father because He is *God from God*, Almighty from Almighty, and being born from the Eternal one is co-eternal with Him; not later in point of time, not lower in power, not unlike in glory, not divided in essence: but at the same time the only begotten of the eternal Father was born eternal of the Holy Spirit and the Virgin Mary. And this nativity which took place in time took nothing from, and added nothing to that divine and eternal birth, but expended

itself wholly on the restoration of man who had been deceived: in order that he might both vanquish death and overthrow by his strength, the Devil who possessed the power of death. For we should not now be able to overcome the author of sin and death unless He took our nature on Him and made it His own, whom neither sin could pollute nor death retain. Doubtless then, He was conceived of the Holy Spirit within the womb of His Virgin Mother....

And when Matthew speaks of *the Book of the Generation of Jesus Christ, the Son of David, the Son of Abraham*, he might have also sought out the instruction afforded by the statements of the Apostles. And reading in the Epistle to the Romans, *Paul, a servant of Jesus Christ, called an Apostle, separated unto the Gospel of God, which He had promised before by His prophets in the Holy Scripture concerning His Son, who was made unto Him of the seed of David after the flesh*, he might have bestowed a loyal carefulness upon the pages of the prophets. And finding the promise of God who says to Abraham, *In thy seed shall all nations be blest*, to avoid all doubt as to the reference of this seed, he might have followed the Apostle when He says, *To Abraham were the promises made and to his seed. He saith not and to seeds, as if in many, but as if in one, and to thy seed which is Christ*. Isaiah's prophecy also he might have grasped by a closer attention to what he says, *Behold, a virgin shall conceive and bear a Son and they shall call His name Immanuel*, which is interpreted *God with us*. And the same prophet's words he might have read faithfully. *A child is born to us, a Son is given to us, whose power is upon His shoulder, and they shall call His name the Angel of the Great Counsel, Wonderful, Counsellor, the Mighty God, the Prince of Peace, the Father of the age to come.* And then he would not speak so erroneously as to say that the Word became flesh in such a way that Christ, born of the Virgin's womb, had the form of man, but had not the reality of His mother's body. Or is it possible that he thought our Lord Jesus Christ was not of our nature for this reason, that the angel, who was sent to the blessed Mary ever Virgin, says, *The Holy Ghost shall come upon thee and the power of the Most High shall overshadow thee: and therefore that Holy Thing also that shall be born of thee shall be called the Son of God*, on the supposition that as the conception of the Virgin was a Divine act, the flesh of the conceived did not partake of the conceiver's nature? But that birth so uniquely wondrous and so wondrously unique, is not to be understood in such wise that the properties of His kind were removed through the novelty of His creation. For though the Holy Spirit imparted fertility to the Virgin, yet a real body was received from her body....

III. Without detriment therefore to the properties of either nature and substance which then came together in one person, majesty took on humility, strength weakness, eternity mortality: and for the paying off of the debt belonging to our condition inviolable nature was united with possible nature, so that, as suited the needs of our case, one and the same Mediator between God and men, the Man Christ Jesus, could both die with the one and not die with the other.

Thus in the whole and perfect nature of true man was true God born, complete in what was His own, complete in what was ours. And by "ours" we mean what the Creator formed in us from the beginning and what He undertook to repair. For what the Deceiver brought in and man deceived committed, had no trace in the Saviour. Nor, because He partook of man's weaknesses, did He therefore share our faults. He took the form of a slave without stain of sin, increasing the human and not diminishing the divine: because that emptying of Himself whereby the Invisible made Himself visible and, Creator and Lord of all things though He be, wished to be a mortal, was the bending down of pity, not the failing of power. Accordingly He who while remaining in the form of God made man, was also made man in the form of a slave. For both natures retain their own proper character without loss: and as the form of God did not do away with the form of a slave, so the form of a slave did not impair the form of God....

IV. There enters then these lower parts of the world the Son of God, descending from His heavenly home and yet not quitting His Father's glory, begotten in a new order by a new nativity. In a new order, because being invisible in His own nature, He became visible in ours, and He whom nothing could contain was content to be contained: abiding before all time He began to be in time: the Lord of all things, He obscured His immeasurable majesty and took on Him the form of a servant: being God that cannot suffer, He did not disdain to be man that can, and, immortal as He is, to subject Himself to the laws of death. The Lord assumed

His mother's nature without her faultiness: nor in the Lord Jesus Christ, born of the Virgin's womb, does the wonderfulness of His birth make His nature unlike ours. For He who is true God is also true man: and in this union there is no lie, since the humility of manhood and the loftiness of the Godhead both meet there. For as God is not changed by the showing of pity, so man is not swallowed up by the dignity. For each form does what is proper to it with the co-operation of the other; that is the Word performing what appertains to the Word, and the flesh carrying out what appertains to the flesh. One of them sparkles with miracles, the other succumbs to injuries. And as the Word does not cease to be on an equality with His Father's glory, so the flesh does not forego the nature of our race. For it must again and again be repeated that one and the same is truly Son of God and truly son of man. God in that *in the beginning was the Word, and the Word was with God, and the Word was God*; man in that *the Word became flesh and dwelt in us*. God in that a*ll things were made by Him, and without Him was nothing made*: man in that *He was made of a woman, made under law*. The nativity of the flesh was the manifestation of human nature: the childbearing of a virgin is the proof of Divine power. The infancy of a babe is shown in the humbleness of its cradle: the greatness of the Most High is proclaimed by the angels' voices. He whom Herod treacherously endeavours to destroy is like ourselves in our earliest stage: but He whom the Magi delight to worship on their knees is the Lord of all. So too when He came to the baptism of John, His forerunner, lest He should not be known through the veil of flesh which covered

His Divinity, the Father's voice thundering from the sky, said, *This is My beloved Son, in whom I am well pleased*. And thus Him whom the devil's craftiness attacks as man, the ministries of angels serve as God. To be hungry and thirsty, to be weary, and to sleep, is clearly human: but to satisfy 5,000 men with five loaves, and to bestow on the woman of Samaria living water, droughts of which can secure the drinker from thirsting any more, to walk upon the surface of the sea with feet that do not sink, and to quell the risings of the waves by rebuking the winds, is, without any doubt, Divine. Just as therefore, to pass over many other instances, it is not part of the same nature to be moved to tears of pity for a dead friend, and when the stone that closed the four-days' grave was removed, to raise that same friend to life with a voice of command: or, to hang on the cross, and turning day to night, to make all the elements tremble: or, to be pierced with nails, and yet open the gates of paradise to the robber's faith: so it is not part of the same nature to say, *I and the Father are one*, and to say, *the Father is greater than I*. For although in the Lord Jesus Christ God and man is one person, yet the source of the degradation, which is shared by both, is one, and the source of the glory, which is shared by both, is another. For His manhood, which is less than the Father, comes from our side: His Godhead, which is equal to the Father, comes from the Father.

V. Therefore in consequence of this unity of person which is to be understood in both natures, we read of the Son of Man also descending from heaven, when the Son of God took flesh from the Virgin who bore

Him. And again the Son of God is said to have been crucified and buried, although it was not actually in His Divinity whereby the Only-begotten is co-eternal and con-substantial with the Father, but in His weak human nature that He suffered these things. And so it is that in the Creed also we all confess that the Only-begotten Son of God was crucified and buried, according to that saying of the Apostle: *for if they had known, they would never have crucified the Lord of glory.* But when our Lord and Saviour Himself would instruct His disciples' faith by His questionings, He said, *Whom do men say that I, the Son of Man, am?* And when they had put on record the various opinions of other people, He said, *But ye, whom do ye say that I am?* Me, that is, who is the Son of Man, and whom ye see in the form of a slave, and in true flesh, whom do ye say that I am? Whereupon blessed Peter, whose divinely inspired confession was destined to profit all nations, said, *Thou art Christ, the Son of the living God.* And not undeservedly was he pronounced blessed by the Lord, drawing from the chief corner-stone the solidity of power which his name also expresses, he, who, through the revelation of the Father, confessed Him to be at once Christ and Son of God: because the receiving of the one of these without the other was of no avail to salvation, and it was equally perilous to have believed the Lord Jesus Christ to be either only God without man, or only man without God. But after the Lord's resurrection (which, of course, was of His true body, because He was raised the same as He had died and been buried), what else was effected by the forty days' delay than the cleansing of our faith's purity from all darkness? For to that end He talked with

His disciples, and dwelt and ate with them, He allowed Himself to be handled with diligent and curious touch by those who were affected by doubt, He entered when the doors were shut upon the Apostles, and by His breathing upon them gave them the Holy Spirit, and bestowing on them the light of understanding, opened the secrets of the Holy Scriptures. So again He showed the wound in His side, the marks of the nails, and all the signs of His quite recent suffering, saying, *See My hands and feet, that it is I. Handle Me and see that a spirit hath not flesh and bones, as ye see Me have*; in order that the properties of His Divine and human nature might be acknowledged to remain still inseparable: and that we might know the Word not to be different from the flesh, in such a sense as also to confess that the one Son of God is both the Word and flesh. Of this mystery of the faith your opponent Eutyches must be reckoned to have but little sense if he has recognized our nature in the Only-begotten of God neither through the humiliation of His having to die, nor through the glory of His rising again. Nor has he any fear of the blessed apostle and evangelist John's declaration when he says, *every spirit which confesses Jesus Christ to have come in the flesh, is of God: and every spirit which destroys Jesus is not of God, and this is Antichrist*. But what is *to destroy* Jesus, except to take away the human nature from Him, and to render void the mystery, by which alone we were saved, by the most barefaced fictions. The truth is that being in darkness about the nature of Christ's body, he must also be befooled by the same blindness in the matter of His sufferings. For if he does not think the cross of the Lord fictitious, and does not doubt that the punishment He underwent to save the world is likewise true, let him acknowledge the flesh of Him whose death he already believes: and let him not disbelieve Him man with a body like ours, since he acknowledges Him to have been able to suffer: seeing that the denial of His true flesh is also the denial of His bodily suffering. If therefore he receives the Christian faith, and does not turn away his ears from the preaching of the Gospel: let him see what was the nature that hung pierced with nails on the wooden cross, and, when the side of the Crucified was opened by the soldier's spear, let him understand whence it was that blood and water flowed, that the Church of God might be watered from the font and from the cup. Let him hear also the blessed Apostle Peter, proclaiming that the sanctification of the Spirit takes place through the sprinkling of Christ's blood. And let him not read cursorily the same Apostle's words when he says, *Knowing that not with corruptible things, such as silver and gold, have ye been redeemed from your vain manner of life which is part of your fathers' tradition, but with the precious blood of Jesus Christ as of a lamb without spot and blemish.* Let him not resist too the witness of the blessed Apostle John, who says: *and the blood of Jesus the Son of God cleanseth us from all sin.* And again: *this is the victory which overcometh the world, our faith.* And *who is He that overcometh the world save he that believeth that Jesus is the Son of God. This is He that came by water and blood, Jesus Christ: not by water only, but by water and blood. And it is the Spirit that testifieth, because the Spirit is the truth, because there are three that bear witness, the Spirit, the water and the blood, and the three are one.* The Spirit, that is, of sanctification, and the blood of redemption, and the water of baptism: because the three are one, and remain undivided, and none of them is separated from this connection; because the catholic Church lives and progresses by this faith, so that in Christ Jesus neither the manhood without the true Godhead nor the Godhead without the true manhood is believed in.[1]

---

1. In *Nicene and Post-Nicene Fathers*, Second Series, ed. Philip Schaff and Henry Wace, trans. Charles Lett Felto (1895; repr., Peabody, Mass.: Hendrickson, 2004), 12:38–43.

Scripture Index

OLD TESTAMENT
Genesis
1	57–59
1:1	22, 56, 67
1:1–4	57
1:3	56
1:6	56
1:9	56
1:11	56
1:14	56
1:20	56
1:24	56
1:26	56
1:26–27	22, 32, 129
1:31	32
2:7	22, 86
2:17	23
3	8, 152
3:15	23, 28, 89
3:24	14
4:16	14
9:6	32
12:1	25
14:17–24	66
20	152
22:18	90
34	152
40	153
49:1	149

Exodus
3:1–6	10
3:6	65
3:14	112
3:14–15	65
4:22	17
20:3	63
20:8–11	68

Leviticus
16:4–5	154
16:29–34	154

Numbers
24:14	149

Deuteronomy
8:3	14
29:29	12–13, 15, 17

Joshua
1:2	25

2 Samuel
7:12	90

1 Kings
4:21	25
8	153

1 Chronicles
29:11	71

Job
40:10	71

Psalms
2	59
2:6–9	59
2:8	151
8:5	22
33:6	57
40:2	21
40:6	37
45:3–4	59
45:6–7	59
46:8	31, 37
51:1–12	21
51:5	93
89:20	17
89:27	17

SCRIPTURE INDEX

Psalms (*continued*)
104:30   22
110:1   60
132:11   90
144:5   26

Isaiah
2:2   149
6:1–3   60–61
6:1–7   10
6:10   60
7:14   17, 25, 90
9:2   21
9:6   61
11:1   90
35:2   71
40:2–3   61
40:3   61
40:5   61
40:9   61
41:4   70
43:10–11 70
43:11   64, 124
44:6   70
53:1   60
53:4   85
55:8   15n6
55:8–9   13
63:19   26
64:1   26

Jeremiah
17:5–8   124
17:9   21
23:1–6   26
23:20   149
31:9   17
33:15   90

Ezekiel
38:16   149

Daniel
10:14   149

Hosea
3:5   149
11:1   26
13:4   64, 124

Micah
4:1–2   149
5:2   63
5:2–5   26

Malachi
3:1–4   26
3:6   34, 71

NEW TESTAMENT

Matthew
1   83
1:1   90
1:18   94
1:20   30, 37, 94
1:20–21 89
1:21   17, 64
1:23   30, 90
2:2   63
3:1–12   61
4:2   84
4:10   112
7:29   65
8:17   85n6
8:24   84
11:27   72
11:28   155
16:13   135
22:37   7
26:38   86
26:39   98
26:42   98
26:44   98
27:50   86
28:18   71
28:19   135
28:19–20 3
28:20   71

Mark
1:1–11   61
1:3   62
1:9   62
1:22   65
3:5   95
4:38   84
8:12   95
9:36–37 95
13:32   111

Luke
1:35   30, 37, 94
1:42   90
1:47   94
2   82
2:4   83
2:6   83
2:7   64, 89
2:13–14 21
2:21   83
2:40   82–83
2:46–47 65
2:52   82–83
3   83
3:1–22   61
3:22   31
3:38   17

SCRIPTURE INDEX

4:21	65
19:10	135
22:44	84
23:46	86
24:27	65
24:44–47	65

John

1:1	58, 165
1:1–3	152
1:1–4	85
1:1–5	57
1:3	152
1:3–4	58
1:4	125, 131
1:5	21
1:14	24, 30–31, 61, 71, 81, 115, 152
1:18	72, 115, 128
3:13	113, 115n13
3:16	32, 71
3:16–18	120
4:6–7	84
4:24	105
5:8–9	68
5:16–17	68
5:17	116
5:37	65
5:39	10
6:62	113
6:68	14
8:40	83
8:53	65
8:56	65
8:58	65, 112
10:27–30	74
11:35	95
12	60
12:27	95
12:41	60
14:9–10	128
17:3	10, 118
17:4	96
17:4–5	104
17:5	32
19:28	84
19:30	86
20:5	56
20:25	66
20:27–28	54
20:28	66
21:20	58

Acts

1:8	135
1:24	71
2	56
2:22	83
2:30	90
2:42	5
2:44–45	5
3:6	83
4:12	64
7:59	71
13:33	59
18:24	65
20:28	111

Romans

1:3	83, 90
1:18–32	15
1:18–11:33	6
4:25	119
5:14	129, 153
5:15	83
5:15–21	124
8:3	85
8:34	154
9–11	28
9:3	74
9:3–5	39
9:5	74, 90, 113
10:13	71
11:36	152
12:1–15:33	6
12:2	7
15:8	83

1 Corinthians

1:18–31	132
2:8	61, 111
2:11–12	13
8:6	58, 152
9:5	83
11:19	30n15
12	56
13:12	12
15:4	65
15:14	35, 119
15:17	35, 119
15:19	119
15:21	83
15:27	71
15:45	129
15:45–49	153
15:49	130

2 Corinthians

3:18	130
4:3–4	130
4:4	146, 153
5:10	71
5:21	33, 95
8:9	126

Galatians

1:19	83
3:13	33
3:16	83, 90
4:3–5	27
4:4	25, 28, 30, 37, 83, 89, 90
5:20	30n15
6:16	28

Ephesians

1:20	154
1:22	71
1:23	71
2:1	21
4	56
4:4–6	157
4:10	71
4:17–18	21
4:23–24	130
4:24	135

Philippians

2	33
2:5–8	32
2:6–8	33n17, 126
2:7	33, 85
2:8	84
3:21	85

Colossians

1:13	68
1:15	153
1:15–20	68
1:15–23	126
1:16	58, 152
1:16–17	68
1:17	112, 153
2:9	24, 75
3:1	154
3:9–10	130
3:10	7, 135

1 Timothy

1:10	4
2:5	64, 79, 109
3:9	5
3:16	30, 35
4:6	4, 5
6:3	5

2 Timothy

1:10	64
1:13–14	5
3:15	63
4:3	4

Titus

1:1	5
1:4	64
1:9	5
2:1	4
2:13	64
3:6	64

Hebrews

1–2	91
1:1	148
1:1–2	149
1:1–3	148–50
1:2	58, 72, 150
1:2–3	126, 150
1:3	67, 68, 116, 153
1:6	126
1:8	126
1:8–9	60, 74
1:13	154
2	92
2:9–10	92
2:9–17	126
2:10	83
2:10–18	91, 124
2:11	92
2:14	21, 81, 90, 92, 131
2:15	125
2:16	99
2:17	81, 84, 90, 92–93, 99
2:18	83, 99
4:12	10
4:14	100
4:15	81, 88, 90, 95, 100, 124
5:7–10	124
5:8	83
6:17	151
7:3	66
7:14	83, 90
7:25	100, 154
7:26	95
8:1	154
8:2	100
8:6	100
8:13	100
9:11	100
9:14	95
9:22	154
9:23–24	100
10:5	37
10:12	154
11:7	151
12:1	19
12:2	154
13:8	71

SCRIPTURE INDEX

James
1:19	136
3:9	32

1 Peter
1:10–12	10, 30, 56
2:21–23	84
2:22	95
3:15	155

2 Peter
1:1	75
1:11	64
2:1	30n15
2:20	64
3:18	64, 133

1 John
1:1–4	51, 69
2:18	86
2:23	86
3:2	12
3:5	95
3:8	129
4:1	137
4:2–3	51
4:3	86, 145
4:9	51
5:20–21	69

2 John
7	86, 145
9–10	5

Revelation
1:1	23
1:4	71
1:8	21, 69–70
1:12	69
1:12–16	61
1:17	10, 69
1:17–18	70
5:5	83
5:9	136
7:9	19
12:9	23
19:16	71
21:6	70
22:4	12
22:13	70
22:16	83

Confessions Index

Apostles' Creed
Full 157–58

Athanasian Creed
1–44 160–64
22 76
29 120
31 76
31–33 77, 86
34 108
37 108
44 120

Belgic Confession of Faith
Art. 2 15–16
Art. 3 16
Art. 9 165
Art. 10 76–77
Art. 17 23
Art. 18 28, 81, 86, 90, 94, 99
Art. 19 41, 49, 84, 105, 122

Canons of Dort
2.3–2.4 111
2.5 132

Definition of Chalcedon
Whole 164–66

Heidelberg Catechism
Q&A 9 22
Q&A 12–19 123
Q&A 17 124
Q&A 19 23
Q&A 24 157
Q&A 27 67
Q&A 33 32
Q&A 35 95
Q&A 36 122
Q&A 48 114

Nicene Creed
Whole 158–60

Second Helvetic Confession
Ch. 11 95

Thirty-Nine Articles
Art. 2 91

Westminster Confession of Faith
Ch. 1.1 15–16
Ch. 7.1 123
Ch. 8.2 91

Westminster Shorter Catechism
Q&A 1 8